The 10% Differentiator

The perfect book for leaders
to elevate performance

THE

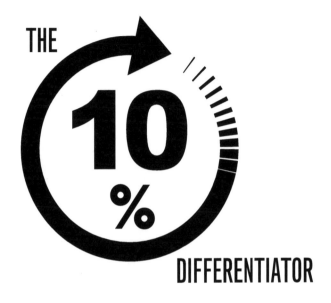

10

%

DIFFERENTIATOR

How to create a connected,
innovative and capable
organisation in the
next 12 months

ANTON VAN DER WALT

Typeset and cover design by BookPOD

ISBN: 978-0-6459654-0-7 (pbk) eISBN: 978-0-6459654-1-4

 A catalogue record for this book is available from the National Library of Australia

This book is a testament to the incredible leaders I've collaborated with and mentored over the years. Several of them have generously shared their invaluable insights, allowing me to weave their wisdom throughout these pages. To all who have contributed, directly or indirectly, to this endeavour, my sincere gratitude.

Contents

Preface

Throughout my interactions with leaders from different backgrounds and roles, a shared set of challenges consistently emerges. This pattern reveals that the challenges are not so much about their core skills or even their tenure in leadership. They are more about the nuances in their interactions that these leaders would very often miss.

These nuances boil down to just a few simple but critical things: building trust, effective communication, and understanding people's value systems, for example. And these small variations got me thinking: what's *really* the difference between those who lead well and those who become exceptional leaders?

In thinking about this issue, I realised that big transformations are not always needed. By focusing on improving just about 10% of their current approach, a leader could experience far greater success.

Think of someone who is seemingly equipped with all the right skills and experience. What is this elusive extra 10% they should consider? It is found in the small but crucial actions: good communication, an encouraging mindset, the effort to value all kinds of feedback and understand others, and an ability to show genuine empathy. Small as they may seem, these actions and behaviours have a deeply profound effect on the quality of leadership.

These observations inspired my research and became the driving force behind this book. Dive into *The 10% Differentiator* to discover how even just a few small shifts in one's thinking and actions can take you from being good to becoming exceptional.

Introduction

'In a busy marketplace,
not standing out is the
same as being invisible.'

– Seth Godin

In the fast-paced and ever-evolving business world, standing still is akin to going backwards. Organisations worldwide tirelessly seek to become more efficient, refine their processes, and maximise their capabilities. Many operate near their peak capacity, often settling in their comfort zone or their familiar space, deeming this as 'satisfactory' or 'good enough'. However, there's always room for improvement, always a next level to aim for.

It's a relentless pursuit of this familiar level, where we know what to do, and how to achieve our objectives. In reality this is where many have come to find a comfortable, albeit sometimes complacent, sense of equilibrium. But what if I told you that the real potential for transformative growth and success lies beyond this level? This is where I introduce the concept of the '10% Differentiator'.

Many senior executives and leaders find themselves effectively working within this 'adequate' or 'good enough' realm, leveraging their industry knowledge, financial expertise, and administrative management skills. It is a familiar space. Yet, the pressing question remains: what lies beyond 'good enough'? What separates the 'good' from the 'outstanding'? What if we could unlock and harness an extra 10%? Think about these possibilities.

More than ever before, we are witnessing a shift in the skillsets required of senior executives. No longer can they rely solely on their industry expertise or administrative capabilities. We are moving towards a business landscape characterised by tech-centric operations, a diverse workforce, and higher public scrutiny. Today's leaders must be adept communicators, relationship builders, and people-oriented problem solvers.[1]

What is this 10% Differentiator?

The 10% Differentiator is not about a quantifiable numerical increase in performance or skill. Rather, it symbolises the additional capacity that a leader requires to drive an organisation, manage a project, or oversee a department beyond the accepted norm, beyond the 'adequate' level that we have grown accustomed to. It represents the unique attributes or processes that can propel you from being 'good enough' to achieving 'excellence'.

This concept pushes organisations out of their comfort zones, challenging the status quo and nurturing an innovative, courageous, and resilient culture. It calls for leaders to transcend the realm of familiarity and predictability and to explore the challenging, but potentially transformative, territory of the 10% Differentiator.

In the following chapters of this book, we delve into the heart of the 10% Differentiator. We provide real life case studies, research-based strategies, and actionable advice, all designed to help you unlock and harness this transformative potential.

We explore the roles of diversity, inclusive leadership, collaboration, continuous learning, and technological adaptation in achieving this 10% Differentiator. We also examine how the business landscape, in the aftermath of the global pandemic, necessitates a shift towards becoming more connected, innovative, and capable.

> Are you ready to discover the power of your '10%'? To unlock the potential that could catapult your organisation from good to great, from capable to extraordinary.

This book is a roadmap to your organisation's unique 10% Differentiator. A roadmap that will guide you from the familiar, the comfortable, the 'good enough' to the transformative world of the 10% Differentiator.

It is a journey of continuous learning, of relentless pursuit of excellence, of daring to venture into uncharted territories. Are you ready to discover the power of your '10%'? To unlock the potential that could catapult your organisation from good to great, from capable to extraordinary.

Welcome to the world of the 10% Differentiator. Your journey to creating a connected, innovative, and capable organisation in the next twelve months starts here. Let's dive into this journey together and explore a world where every endeavour, no matter how small, can become a game-changer. Welcome to your future of organisational excellence.

Change

Change is a part of every organisation and when you're working towards increasing your 10% Differentiator, change is inevitable. To embrace your own growth, and the growth of your organisation, you, your superiors, and your team also need the skills to embrace change.

When it comes to your own change you will need to be willing to make the amendments to your own leadership processes, systems, and mindsets in order to become a more effective and high-performing leader. When it comes to change within your organisation, as a leader

> When you're working towards increasing your 10% Differentiator, change is inevitable.

you need to, first, understand the noise that change can create, second, focus on stakeholder engagement, and third, develop your own leadership decency to manage the process well.

Change Can Create Noise

*'There is nothing more difficult
to take in hand, more perilous
to conduct, or more uncertain
in its success, than to take
the lead in the introduction
of a new order of things.'*

– Niccolo Machiavelli

Every organisation experiences what is commonly referred to as 'noise'. This noise is the chatter, gossip, or rumours that circulate in the workplace, particularly during periods of change. The question for leaders is: *are you a part of the problem, contributing to the noise, or are you part of the solution, helping to mitigate it*? As a leader, your role is crucial in managing this noise, ensuring it doesn't disrupt productivity or morale.

Understanding the noise

To address the 'noise', we first need to understand its source. Change in organisations, be it in policies, leadership, or direction – and there will inevitably be change when working towards your 10% Differentiator – often leads to uncertainty and anxiety.

Uncertainty creates a void of information, and in this void of information, employees may create narratives to make sense of what's happening which are far from the truth. This can give birth to rumours, gossip, and false stories which, when left unchecked, can affect the organisation's health and productivity.

Role of leadership in managing noise

Your leadership plays a critical role in controlling the 'noise'. By providing clear, timely, and consistent communication, leaders can help allay fears and keep the rumour mill at bay. Let's delve into practical strategies leaders can employ to effectively manage workplace noise:

> Your leadership plays a critical role in controlling the 'noise'. By providing clear, timely, and consistent communication, leaders can help allay fears and keep the rumour mill at bay.

1. **Clear communication**: Be transparent and clear about changes happening in the organisation. Ambiguity breeds speculation, and speculation often leads to gossip. When people know what's going on, there's less room for rumours.

2. **Two-way dialogue**: Foster a culture where employees feel comfortable voicing their concerns or questions. Listening to their apprehensions, and providing

appropriate responses, can prevent miscommunication and misinformation from spreading.

3. **Regular updates**: Regularly updating your team not only keeps everyone on the same page but also reduces the chance of gossip and rumours. Remember, the absence of accurate information often leads to the circulation of inaccurate information.

4. **Lead by example**: Refuse to participate in gossip. If someone approaches you with rumours, respond by steering the conversation towards facts or productive discussion. By setting this precedent, you encourage others to do the same.

5. **Foster a positive environment**: A positive workplace culture that emphasises respect, collaboration, and open communication can help curb the spread of noise. When employees trust their leaders and each other, they are less likely to engage in gossip.

6. **Training and development**: Train managers and employees on the impact of workplace gossip and the importance of respectful communication. Equip them with the tools and knowledge to navigate changes effectively.

7. **Recognition and reward**: Recognise and reward behaviour that fosters a positive work environment. This could be as simple as praising an employee for their professionalism or rewarding a team for their excellent communication during a challenging project.

8. **Encourage team building**: Activities that build camaraderie and trust among team members can help reduce gossip. A team that values and trusts each other is less likely to participate in harmful chatter.

Managing 'noise' in the workplace is a vital aspect of the 10% leader. By creating an open, communicative, and respectful work environment, leaders can significantly reduce the spread of harmful gossip and rumours.

The goal is not to silence all chatter – that's both impossible and undesirable. Rather, it's about ensuring that the communication within your organisation is positive, productive, and rooted in fact. This approach, when integrated into the organisational culture, can lead to a healthier, happier, and more productive workplace.

'One of the most common ways to overcome resistance to change is to educate people about it beforehand. Communication of ideas helps people see the need for and the logic of a change. The education process can involve one-on-one discussions, presentations to groups, or memos and reports.'

– John P. Kotter

Building Critical Stakeholder Engagement

*'The most important thing
in communication is to
hear what is not said.'*

– Peter F. Drucker

In the initial stages of my leadership journey, I held the position of Manager of Industrial Relations for a prominent automobile manufacturing conglomerate. Stationed in South Africa, the complexities of interfacing with trade unions frequently came to the forefront. A primary challenge in my role was overseeing change management. Within the factory setting, adjustments such as modifying the manufacturing line speed, introducing overtime protocols, or reassigning employees to different stations were common. While these modifications might appear minor, navigating them alongside trade unions made them intricate endeavours.

This is where I learned that stakeholder engagement is crucial to the success of any change management initiative. An essential aspect of change management is understanding the perspectives and needs of all stakeholders. Often, individuals resist change because they feel excluded from the decision-making process.

To overcome this hurdle, it's vital to create a space for dialogue.

Stakeholders need to understand the rationale behind the proposed change, the benefits it brings, and the impact on them. Importantly, they must also have the opportunity to voice their concerns and suggestions.

By involving stakeholders in the change process, we acknowledge their value and foster a sense of ownership and commitment. This doesn't mean everyone will support the proposed change, but their involvement increases the chance of acceptance, reduces resistance, and makes the transition smoother.

'Effective CEOs are clearly visionary, strong communicators and culture builders. However, one thing that sets great CEOs apart is that they are decisive. They don't make decisions in a vacuum or believe that their way is always the best way. Rather, they engage in open dialogues, gather information, and listen to many points of view. Then, they make tough decisions for the organization.'

– Edith Onderick-Harvey,
NextBridge Consulting, LLC

Effective tools and mechanisms for change management

1. **Change management models:** Various models can guide the change management process. Kurt Lewin's Unfreeze-Change-Refreeze model[2] and John Kotter's 8-Step Process for Leading Change[3] are among the most popular. These models provide a structured approach to change, emphasising the importance of communication, stakeholder engagement, and iterative learning.

2. **Communication plan**: A well-crafted communication plan is integral to successful change management. It ensures that relevant information is consistently shared across the organisation, addresses concerns and misconceptions, and enables open dialogue.

3. **Feedback mechanisms**: Tools like surveys, focus groups, or town hall meetings can be used to gather feedback and suggestions. These mechanisms provide valuable insights that can help refine the change strategy and make it more acceptable to the stakeholders.

4. **Training and support systems**: Changes often require stakeholders to learn new skills or adapt to new roles. Providing the necessary training and support can ease this transition and show the organisation's commitment to their success.

5. **Monitoring and evaluation**: Regular monitoring and evaluation can help identify potential issues, measure progress, and assess the impact of change. This process is essential for learning and improvement, allowing the organisation to refine its change management practices over time.

Change management is a complex and challenging process, but with the right approach and tools, it's possible to increase the likelihood of success. It requires thoughtful planning, effective communication, stakeholder engagement, and a commitment to continuous learning and improvement. By recognising and addressing these factors, leaders can implement change that is not only accepted but also embraced by those involved.

Decency in Leadership: Balancing Compassion and Accountability

'When the norm is decency,
other virtues can thrive:
integrity, honesty, compassion,
kindness, and trust.'

– Raja Krishnamoorthi

Balancing decency and success in leadership can often seem like a precarious tightrope. But the ability to do so is vital. While being a decent leader is particularly necessary during times of change and transformation, it is something that is needed for effective leadership at all times. In fact, along with intellect and emotional intelligence, experts identify decency as the third important trait for leaders.[4]

However, it's not always easy to incorporate decency into leadership. Many leaders who tend to be compassionate, kind, and people-orientated, often grapple with the thought that their decency and compassion are being mistaken for leniency, allowing them to be taken advantage of. Should they then adopt a more aggressive demeanour to be effective?

The misconception of decency in leadership

There's a common misconception that leaders must be hard-nosed, aggressive, and even ruthless to be successful. Leaders who are naturally empathetic and compassionate often find themselves questioning their approach, comparing themselves to more assertive counterparts. This comparison can lead to a problematic path where they may feel compelled to change their nature to fit a stereotypical mould of leadership.

However, trying to emulate a leadership style that doesn't align with one's nature can lead to inauthenticity, causing dissonance between the leader and their team. Authenticity in leadership is crucial for building trust, respect, and credibility among team members. It is important, therefore, for leaders to remain true to their nature while also cultivating a healthy culture of accountability.

> *'One of the criticisms I've faced over the years is that I'm not aggressive enough or assertive enough or maybe somehow because I'm empathetic, it means I'm weak. I totally rebel against that. I refuse to believe that you cannot be both compassionate and strong.'*
>
> – Jacinda Ardern, 40th Prime Minister of New Zealand

Balancing decency and accountability

One of the key mechanisms ensuring a balance between decency and accountability is implementing robust governance processes. Governance, in this context, refers to the systems, processes, and metrics put in place to measure performance, track deliverables, and hold individuals accountable.

Leaders who struggle with maintaining boundaries due to their compassionate nature can benefit significantly from these processes. For instance, regular meetings where team members report on their progress, or a well-defined system to track and review key performance indicators (KPIs), can provide a structured way to monitor performance and hold people accountable. Either makes it clear that performance expectations are non-negotiable and must be met, irrespective of the leader's compassionate disposition.

The power of process

The implementation of clear processes can help alleviate many of the issues faced by compassionate leaders. Here are a few mechanisms that could be employed:

1. **Weekly reporting**: Implementing a weekly reporting system where each team member updates their progress against set KPIs helps keep track of their performance.
2. **Performance reviews**: Regular performance reviews

provide an opportunity to give constructive feedback and address issues directly, without aggression or bias.

3. **Standard operating procedures (SOPs):** Creating SOPs for regular tasks can standardise performance expectations and provide a clear framework for accountability.

4. **Team meetings**: Regular team meetings offer a forum for open communication, ensuring everyone is aligned on goals and expectations.

5. **Feedback mechanisms**: An environment where everyone feels comfortable giving and receiving feedback can help alleviate issues for compassionate leaders. This can be accomplished through feedback tools, regular one-on-one sessions, or anonymous feedback systems.

6. **Mentoring**: Creating the opportunity for true mentoring will help compassionate leaders deliver growth opportunities to their staff that will allow them to increase their own performance over time. This benefits both the staff and the organisation as a whole, and supports the increased demands that can occur during change.

Maintaining decency while implementing governance

While implementing these governance processes, leaders must ensure they maintain their compassionate demeanour, a particular challenge during change. It is essential to communicate clearly with the team that these processes are not designed to curb their freedom or creativity, but rather to ensure fairness, accountability, and high performance. This can be achieved through regular communication, transparent discussions, and an open-door policy.

> Decency in leadership does pay in business. It fosters a culture of trust, respect, and mutual understanding.

Decency in leadership does pay in business. It fosters a culture of trust, respect, and mutual understanding. By combining their inherent compassion with robust governance processes, leaders can ensure accountability without compromising their decency.

Individual Leadership Growth

In my tenure as a leader, I've recognised the importance of self-awareness. Understanding one's strengths and weaknesses not only creates the opportunity for personal growth but also bolsters the organisation as a whole. Genuine organisational change is spearheaded by leaders who are introspective, yet willing to listen to and accept external feedback. They view challenges as transformative opportunities rather than mere hurdles.

The modern business environment is marked by swift evolutions, which renders traditional authoritative roles insufficient. Effective leadership now requires a shift from authority-based power to a more influential and collaborative approach. Traditional authority is rooted in position, ego, and directive strategies. In contrast, influential leadership emphasises collaboration, inspiration, and a personal touch. To navigate this distinction, leaders must embark on a journey of self-reflection and continuous learning. This commitment to personal growth not only enhances individual capabilities but also elevates the entire organisation.

Years ago, one of my mentors said to me, 'There are two reasons why people change. They see the light (become aware), or they feel the heat.' Cultivating self-awareness is not an instantaneous feat; it's a continuous endeavour. This self-awareness is critical for several reasons. It's indicative of potential success, foundational to emotional intelligence, boosts confidence, and necessitates genuine introspection. Committing to this path allows leaders to adapt and evolve in alignment with their core values.

The 10% Differentiator in Action

Embracing and supporting change effectively as a leader is a difficult task, but one that will help you gain that 10% Differentiator. This will look different for every leader depending on your business, your organisation, your staff, and even your specific project. Getting it right will see you heading from good to exceptional, and being able to recognise when you're getting it right is a vital first step.

Here are some real life examples of the 10% Differentiator in action with leaders who are working to effect their own change or transformation.

Leadership mentorship: lessons from coaching with Andrew Almeida

'Reflecting on my professional journey thus far, the role of mentors has remained consistently paramount. Initially, my focus was on replicating their methods, but as I advanced and recognised the uniqueness of each individual's approach, my goal transformed. Today, I strive to extract inspirational elements from their teachings and incorporate those into my approach and career trajectory.

The knowledge I've garnered presents itself as distinct pockets, each containing its own brilliance. What has been immensely beneficial from these engaging interactions, is the ability to connect these separate entities of knowledge. By assimilating what I've learned from various mentors, approaches, situations, and encounters, I'm beginning to shape my leadership identity holistically, as opposed to being only proficient in discrete areas.

Regarding these mentoring sessions, I genuinely appreciate their conversational nature, free from rigid agendas. The preparatory dialogues, with their questions and responses, serve as the foundation for further discussions. I find this format especially engaging, as it's not always led by the mentor. At times, I would steer the conversation, prompting inquiries from my mentor, at other times, they would take the lead. This fluidity fosters a higher level of engagement than a typical agenda-driven meeting.

By actively participating, I'm able to extract more value, particularly from key messages. These insights have proven to be significantly useful in other areas of my career, particularly around topics such as control, expressing values, feedback, and cultivating an effective organisational culture.'

Andrew Almeida – Head of Operations

Key takeaways from Andrew are:

1. **Value of mentorship**: He has learned how to draw on the valuable experiences, knowledge and lessons of his mentors to implement change in his own leadership. Instead of just replicating their methods, Andrew distils the inspirational elements from each mentor and incorporates them into his unique leadership style with the result that he has become a more effective leader than before.

2. **Holistic approach**: Andrew takes the wisdom from his mentors and situations and connects them as a cohesive whole. This has helped him become more well-rounded, enabling him to apply his skills across various aspects of leadership, rather than just being good at specific tasks.

3. **Importance of engagement**: He has found value in the active and dynamic participation in discussions as opposed to simply sitting through a meeting. This kind of engagement helps Andrew extract more value from his sessions and become more involved in the process of learning.

4. **Application of values**: He has learned the importance of leadership values such as control, feedback, and building a positive culture. He sees these as essential elements to be applied in their professional context to continue his growth as a leader.

From engineer to manager to leader: lessons from coaching with Fatma Alashey

'I aspire to continually cultivate an open-minded perspective in business, particularly regarding effective people management strategies and best practices. I'm enthusiastic about mastering a range of skills, especially leveraging empathy to attain set objectives, a practice that has had a significant impact on me in the past four months.

My focus has increasingly been drawn towards understanding control and its role in business situations. This journey has fundamentally altered my approach, teaching me to distinguish between what's within my sphere of control and what isn't. For instance, I've realized that external factors like traffic conditions are beyond my control, but how I respond, perhaps by intelligently using Google Maps to identify less congested routes, is entirely up to me.

From the onset of my career as an engineer, I've been conditioned to think in a certain way: there's a process, and we need to stick to it. But my recent exposure to management has altered this perception. I've come to appreciate the value of soft skills, like empathy, effective communication, and explaining the 'why' behind certain

> *processes. These strategies have proven instrumental in helping people understand what can be accomplished and what constraints we might face.'*
>
> **Fatma Alashey – Service Operations Manager**

Key takeaways from Fatma are:

1. The importance of having an **open mind** in business.
2. How to better manage people through **empathy and understanding**.
3. The necessity of **differentiating between elements within and outside of her control**.
4. The utility of **intelligently navigating uncontrollable situations**, as exemplified by using Google Maps during heavy traffic.
5. The value of **explaining the rationale** behind business processes and operations, aiding in team understanding and cooperation.

Conclusion

Embracing change in your own leadership, and understanding and supporting change within your staff and organisation, is the overarching mindset you need to begin elevating your own 10% Differentiator. It will also put you in the right position to embrace the other elements that will drive you from good to great, including culture.

Culture

The culture you create in your workplace, within your team and organisation, and even in your own mindset, is a vital part of moving from good enough to extraordinary. Research shows that a high-performance culture improves the happiness of staff[5], overall productivity[6], talent attraction and retention[7], and even profits[8]. But it's also a vital part of moving into your 10% Differentiator.

A focus on your culture needs to

> The culture you create in your workplace, within your team and organisation, and even in your own mindset, is a vital part of moving from good enough to extraordinary.

encompass both your team, and your own leadership culture, as well as anything that might hold you back from doing these well.

Building Effective Teams: Understanding, Managing, and Enhancing Performance

'In the long history of humankind (and animal kind, too) those who learned to collaborate and improvise most effectively have prevailed.'

– Charles Darwin

The adage, 'You are only as good as your team' captures the essence of leadership and the essence of your workplace culture. Navigating team dynamics, understanding individuals' strengths and weaknesses, and making tough personnel decisions are all part of the leadership role.

An effective leader must analyse their team's performance, identify who is driving progress, and decide how to handle those not meeting expectations. This task is as complex as it is vital, and

> An effective leader must analyse their team's performance, identify who is driving progress, and decide how to handle those not meeting expectations.

it demands a keen understanding of people, along with the courage to act. This expanded discourse sets the expectations within your team, creates the culture that your team is built around, and provides additional insight into team management and the development of high-performing, diverse teams.

Assessing team performance

When you inherit a new team, your first task is to understand its dynamics and evaluate individual and collective performance. This process involves:

- **Observing the team in action**: Pay attention to interactions, communication styles, and how conflicts are resolved.
- **Reviewing performance data**: Look at past performance reviews, productivity metrics, and feedback from other teams.
- **Conducting individual meetings**: Personal interaction is crucial. These meetings can provide insights into each team member's skills, aspirations, and concerns, and it gives you an opportunity to reinforce the culture you want to build.

Handling underperformers

When you identify underperformers, it's crucial to act promptly yet thoughtfully. The course of action should be based on the individual's circumstances:

- **Training and support**: If the underperformance stems from a skills gap or lack of clarity about the role, provide the necessary training and support.

- **Role realignment**: If the individual's skills don't match their current role but could be valuable elsewhere, consider a role change. The strongest team culture is the one where the right staff are in the right roles.

- **Letting go**: If underperformance persists despite interventions, it may be necessary for the individual to leave the team. Having underperformers on the team will lower morale and bring down the rest of the team culture.

Enriching the team with diversity

When you have an opportunity to bring in new people, resist the temptation to select individuals like yourself. Instead, keep in mind the overall culture of your team. Look for and value diversity which fosters innovation, improves decision-making, and boosts performance.

Here's how to create and manage diverse teams:

- **Hire for diversity**: Seek a mix of backgrounds, perspectives, skills, and experiences when recruiting new team members.

- **Encourage open communication**: Foster a culture where everyone feels comfortable sharing their ideas and opinions.

- **Facilitate inclusive decision-making**: Create a culture (with the systems and processes to support that culture) that ensures everyone has a voice in the decision-making process.
- **Promote cultural competence**: Train your team on diversity and inclusion best practices and encourage understanding and respect for individual differences.

Leadership that puts its focus on culture involves ongoing team assessment and the willingness to make tough decisions when necessary. Managing underperformers and promoting diversity are not easy tasks, but they are necessary for building and leading a high-performing culture and team. As a leader, your success is intrinsically tied to your team's success, so invest time and effort into understanding, managing, and enhancing your team.

'You can't forget that organizational success flows from the hearts and minds of the men and women you lead. Rather than treating your people as you'd like to be treated, treat them as they would like to be treated. Small gestures like opting for face-to-face meetings or sending personal notes can have an enormous impact on teams and their morale.'

– Marillyn Hewson[9]

Accountability: Cultivating a Culture of Responsibility in Leadership

'The price of greatness
is responsibility.'

– Winston Churchill

A cornerstone of successful leadership is accountability – a recurrent theme in my conversations with leaders worldwide. They often grapple with situations where team members do not deliver as expected, raising the crucial question, *'How can I foster a stronger sense of accountability among my team members?'*

To answer this, I draw on personal experience from my early years as a manager in an automotive manufacturing facility.

In the manufacturing sector, accountability is pivotal. A vehicle cannot be assembled in a haphazard fashion. There is a specific sequence to be followed – a clear, defined process with no room for improvisation. I have a clear memory of my training in lean manufacturing. One of the key parts of this learning experience was spending time on the factory floor, getting hands-on experience assembling vehicles. It wasn't always easy – some of the parts looked so similar that it was hard to tell them apart. Thank goodness for the attentive supervisors who were there to guide me. They made sure I didn't accidentally leave out any parts or use the wrong ones in the assembly process! This environment taught me invaluable lessons about accountability and delivery.

The 'trust and verify' approach was critical here. While people were trusted to do their job consistently, robust measurable controls verifying that each step had been completed correctly were implemented. This concept of 'trust and verify' has remained with me and has shaped my own views on accountability.

Understanding accountability

Accountability extends beyond merely holding individuals responsible for tasks. It involves creating a culture where team members understand their roles, commit to their responsibilities, and deliver on their promises. This environment encourages proactive behaviour, open communication, and continuous improvement.

> Leaders can inspire accountability by setting clear expectations, promoting transparency, and empowering team members.

Leaders can inspire accountability by setting clear expectations, promoting transparency, and empowering team members. By defining roles, responsibilities, and objectives clearly, everyone understands what is expected of them, and why their role is so crucial to the team's success.

Encouraging open communication about progress, challenges, and results prevents misunderstandings and builds trust. Empowering individuals, giving them the autonomy to decide how to achieve their objectives, boosts engagement and fosters a sense of ownership.

Establishing governance structures

When it comes to fostering accountability, you can't merely encourage it and expect it to happen. Instead, a robust governance structure is critical. This provides a framework for regular discussions about objectives, progress, and obstacles. It facilitates open conversations, feedback, and assistance where needed.

Effective governance structures can be established by:

- **Implementing regular check-ins:** Regular meetings serve as platforms for discussing progress, identifying bottlenecks, and re-evaluating objectives.
- **Utilising project management tools:** These track tasks, deadlines, and progress, enhancing visibility and accountability.
- **Facilitating open dialogue:** Encouraging team members to express concerns, ask for assistance, or suggest improvements cultivates an open and accountable environment.

Leveraging metrics to monitor progress

As in the manufacturing facility where measurable controls are pivotal, metrics play a crucial role in fostering accountability in any team. They provide a quantifiable way to measure progress, identify areas for improvement, and recognise accomplishments.

In a vehicle manufacturing plant, manufacturing teams create what they call a 'master schedule'. This is a comprehensive plan that visually displays key production metrics and activities over a set period. This schedule ensures streamlined production and optimal resource allocation. It provides a clear view of the production process, from volume and lead times to resource deployment. By coordinating various production activities, the master schedule helps in efficient forecasting, identifying potential bottlenecks, and ensuring smooth operations throughout the production cycle.

Can you imagine a vehicle manufacturing plant that doesn't have a master schedule? It can lead to a lack of coordination in production, inefficient use of resources, and challenges in meeting demand. This disorganisation will result in increased costs, difficulty in forecasting future needs, and a potential decrease in product quality. Essentially, without a master schedule, the manufacturing process can face significant inefficiencies and disruptions, compromising both the production rate and the quality of vehicles.

In the same way, leaders in any industry can leverage metrics by establishing KPIs, using dashboards, and celebrating success. KPIs should be SMART (specific, measurable, achievable, relevant, and time-bound) and monitor progress towards objectives. Dashboards provide a visual representation of progress and give an overview of team performance. Recognising and rewarding achievements boosts morale and encourages further accountability.

Accountability does not happen by chance. It is an outcome of clear expectations, robust governance structures, and reliable metrics. These strategies enable leaders to foster a culture of accountability, ensuring team members consistently deliver on their promises, driving team success. A leader's role isn't about micromanaging; it's about paving the way for the team to succeed and thrive.

> Accountability does not happen by chance. It is an outcome of clear expectations, robust governance structures, and reliable metrics.

Facing Fears in the Executive Suite: Overcoming Imposter Syndrome, Fear of Failure, and Decision Paralysis

'I've missed more than 9,000 shots in my career. I've lost almost 300 games. Twenty-six times I've been trusted to take the game-winning shot and missed. I've failed over and over and over again in my life. And that is why I succeed.'

– Michael Jordan

When it comes to building a robust high-performing culture in your organisation, there are things that can hold you back. A fear of failure and imposter syndrome can lead to decision paralysis, and they can stop you from having the confidence to create a culture that provides both yourself and your team actionable opportunities for growth and success.

Imposter syndrome unveiled

Senior executives and business leaders operate in a high-stakes environment where success is both a goal and a standard. The upper echelons of corporate structures carry with them the expectation of competence, confidence, and leadership acumen. Underneath the poised exterior, often resides an unspoken fear – the so-called 'imposter syndrome'.

Imposter syndrome is a psychological pattern where individuals doubt their accomplishments and have a persistent internalised fear of being exposed as a fraud. This worry about delivering results, a fear about decision-making impacts, and the persistent whisper of self-doubt – 'What if I'm found out?' – are common among high achievers, CEOs, MDs, and senior executives. Despite their success, they may feel undeserving of their position and live with a constant fear of being unmasked.

Coupled with the dread of not delivering expected results and the concern about the effects of their decisions, imposter syndrome can cause significant stress and self-imposed pressure. Understanding the roots of this fear and learning effective ways to manage it can bolster self-confidence and improve performance.

> *'I always did something I was a little not ready to do. I think that's how you grow. When there's that moment of "Wow, I'm not really sure I can do this," and you push through those moments, that's when you have a breakthrough.'*
>
> – Marissa Mayer

How to overcome imposter syndrome

1. **Normalise the fear**: The first step is to recognise that you're not alone. These fears and insecurities are common among people in high-stakes roles. Many successful leaders grapple with the same doubts. Realising this can be a significant relief, minimising the self-imposed stigma associated with such fears.

2. **Self-awareness**: Understanding that these fears are often self-created is crucial. They represent a narrative we've built in our minds, not an objective reality. Developing self-awareness helps identify these patterns of negative thinking, setting the stage for altering this narrative.

3. **Trust in your abilities**: You've earned your position through hard work, skills, and experience. Trust in your abilities and in the people who saw potential in you to assign you the role. They wouldn't have entrusted you with this position if they did not believe in your capabilities.

4. **Focus on what you can control**: Fear often stems from the unknown and the uncontrollable. Refocus your energy on aspects that are within your control, such as your dedication, learning efforts, and your decision-making processes.

5. **Practise self-compassion**: Allow yourself to be human, to make mistakes, and to learn from them. A perfect

track record isn't realistic or sustainable. What matters is your ability to learn, adapt, and grow.

6. **Seek feedback and mentorship**: Regular feedback can help keep imposter syndrome in check by providing an external, more objective view of your performance. Also, consider seeking a mentor who's experienced similar situations. They can provide valuable insights, guidance, and reassurance.

7. **Professional help**: In cases where imposter syndrome leads to significant distress, hinders performance, or creates a less than optimal culture in your workplace, consider seeking help from a professional coach or psychologist. They can provide effective strategies to manage these feelings and enhance self-esteem.

Imposter syndrome can be a significant hurdle in the path of a leader's success, but it's not an insurmountable one. Addressing these fears head-on, acknowledging their prevalence, and developing effective strategies to combat them are crucial steps towards cultivating a healthier mindset and a more resilient leadership style.

Remember, it's not about eliminating all fear or doubt. It's about learning to manage it effectively. You've earned your place. You are indeed good enough, and it's time you believe it. Trust yourself, trust your abilities, and let that guide you in your leadership journey. After all, success in leadership relies not just on abilities but on believing in those abilities.

Fear of not delivering results – fear of failure

The fear of not delivering results or failing is another common worry among senior executives. The pressure to meet targets, expectations, and timelines can be overwhelming, leading to excessive stress and even decision paralysis.

How to tackle this fear:

- Set realistic and achievable goals.
- Develop a clear action plan with contingency plans.
- Embrace failure as a learning opportunity.
- Promote a culture that views failure as a stepping stone to success.
- Regularly review and adjust goals.

Fear of decision impact – anxiety about consequences

Senior executives and leaders also often fear the consequences of their decisions, especially since their choices can significantly influence the organisation's direction and impact many individuals. This fear can lead to indecisiveness or overly cautious decision-making which can then impact the culture of the organisation as a whole.

To manage this fear:

- Ensure thorough data analysis and research before decision-making.

- Encourage open discussions and diverse viewpoints in decision-making processes.

- Consider the potential consequences and prepare mitigation strategies.

- Regularly review and assess decisions to learn from the outcomes.

- Cultivate emotional intelligence to manage the impact of decisions.

Fear in leadership is not a weakness; it is a reality. Even the most seasoned executives grapple with fears. The key lies in acknowledging these fears, understanding their roots, and actively implementing strategies with which to address them.

Remember, being in a leadership position is a testament to your competence and potential. Self-doubt, fear of failure, and decision anxiety are merely hurdles along the way, not insurmountable barriers. Trust in your abilities, learn from your experiences, and navigate your leadership journey with resilience and adaptability.

The 10% Differentiator in Action

Having a culture that supports your ability – and your organisation's ability – to embrace that 10% Differentiator is an important overarching element. Self-awareness and emotional intelligence are big parts of embracing that cultural change that will lead to a journey of growth.

The importance of self-awareness: lessons from coaching with Graham Tunks

'Reflecting on my journey, I've observed a significant expansion in my perspective, yielding a more comprehensive worldview. In retrospect, I acknowledge that I began with a somewhat restricted mindset and lacked empathy. This journey has not only enlightened me about others' experiences but has also led to greater self-awareness, enabling me to strive for betterment and cultivate trust more effectively.

A standout incident that underlines my personal growth pertains to a challenging relationship with a colleague. We had severe disagreements when I initially started this developmental journey. However, with persistent focus and mutual efforts, we've transformed this adversarial relationship into a strong friendship.

My belief in the power of external coaching is unwavering. I think an individual can achieve a certain level of success independently, but to extract that extra 10% — the difference between good and great — requires a skilled outside perspective. Regardless of the field you're in, this small yet crucial percentage requires additional support, which only a select few manage to attain on their own.

Although I believe I have yet to reach that top 10%, I feel a noticeable improvement in myself, even if it's just a few percent. The journey continues, and the critical point is that I can see tangible changes, not only in my operations and self-understanding but also in managing challenges.

The issue with the staff member I mentioned earlier is a prime example. This situation was a daunting challenge, and I initially felt ill-equipped to navigate it. However, with assistance and guidance, I've managed to invert this issue, transforming it into a substantial positive. Without these tools and support, my old approach would have been to cut ties and move on. Now, I have the capacity to turn problems into opportunities.'

Graham Tunks – Commercial Director

Key takeaways from Graham are:

1. The value of a culture of an **open mindset and empathy** in professional relationships.
2. The importance of **self-awareness** and its role in personal and professional growth.
3. The ability to **transform adversarial relationships** into strong, positive connections.
4. The **significance of external coaching** in driving further development and pushing past perceived limitations.

Emotional Intelligence is a valuable skill set: lessons from coaching with Mark Timms

'Coaching has allowed me to see things from a new perspective, essentially training me to adopt alternative viewpoints and enabling me to handle uncomfortable areas with newfound ease. This benefited both my personal growth and my team's management. I used to avoid dealing with emotionally charged situations, both in and outside of work. Now I am more comfortable with such circumstances.

I've honed my emotional intelligence and become adept at managing emotional scenarios both in my personal life and at work. This newfound emotional acuity has facilitated better understanding of my team as individuals and helped me better navigate their emotional responses to both professional and personal events. With the significant amount of change management our business has undergone, my enhanced emotional intelligence has been invaluable in supporting my team through these challenging transitions.

I now realize the value of personal understanding in professional growth. In identifying my initial 90% proficiency, I also discovered a 10% gap, which I have been gradually closing using a Kaizen-like approach. I have incrementally worked on smaller portions, slowly chipping away at this gap. Although I believe it hasn't entirely vanished, I've seen significant progress. This is precisely why I chose to continue with the coaching sessions. They continuously provide me with new insights and perspectives, helping me narrow the remaining gaps.

They have also allowed me to vent my frustrations and concerns in a productive manner. My coach provided an understanding ear, comprehending the nuances of my work, the personalities involved, and the business context. Rather than offering direct solutions, I am guided towards potential coping strategies, thereby facilitating a proactive approach to ongoing challenges. It's immensely beneficial to have someone with whom

> to share these experiences, fostering an even more resilient and adaptable approach to my role as a Managing Director.'
>
> **Mark Timms – MD Commercial Vehicles**

Key takeaways from Mark are:

1. The significance of **understanding one's own character and leadership style** to guide their reactions and responses to various scenarios.

2. The importance of **viewing situations from different perspectives**, allowing for more comprehensive problem-solving and decision-making.

3. The value of **emotional intelligence** in both personal and professional life and its role in understanding and managing team dynamics effectively.

4. The effectiveness of a **Kaizen-like approach** in personal growth, focusing on small, incremental improvements.

5. The benefits of **venting frustrations in a productive culture**, leading to proactive coping strategies and more adaptable problem-solving approaches.

Conclusion

If you're ready to move from good to great and to embrace your own 10% Differentiator, then you must create a culture that embraces that development. This means a culture of team development, leadership accountability, coaching, growth, and opportunity elevation. It also means facing any fears that might be holding you back.

Once you can do that, you're in an excellent place to move to the next element in your journey – balance.

Balance

It may seem counterintuitive, but finding balance in your life is a key part of achieving growth. The reason is because balance brings things into harmony. It lets you embrace ease and flow in both your work and personal life, and that allows you to focus on the opportunities that are already there, waiting for you. These opportunities, however, are easily missed when things are out of balance because you simply aren't able to see beyond your immediate challenges.

> When it comes to finding the balance that can support your own 10% expansion, work-life is only the first part.

When it comes to finding the

balance that can support your own 10% expansion, work-life is only the first part. You also need to consider the balance in leading your team and how to give and embrace feedback in a balanced manner.

Redefining Work-Life Balance

'I believe that being successful
means having a balance of
success stories across the many
areas of your life. You can't
truly be considered successful
in your business life if your
home life is in a shambles.'

– Zig Ziglar

In the corporate world, work-life balance is often espoused as a critical goal for employee satisfaction and retention.[10] Yet, for senior executives and leaders, this balance can seem elusive, if not downright non-existent. The pervasive question is, 'Can there truly be a work-life balance at this level, or is it just work?'

Rethinking the paradigm

The traditional understanding of work-life balance has often been about drawing a clear demarcation between work and personal life. It's about allotting specific periods of the day for work and reserving the rest for family, hobbies, and personal time. However, this rigid compartmentalisation might not always be practical or even beneficial, particularly for those in high-level executive roles.

As a 24/7 individual, you carry the same persona, the same thoughts, and the same challenges whether at work or at home. Life does not come segmented into 'work time' and 'personal time'. Thus, the attempt to disconnect completely from work while at home or vice versa can be a source of stress rather than a stress-reliever.

A new perspective: balanced work-life integration

Consider an alternative, more balanced, perspective – work-life integration. This perspective acknowledges that our work and personal lives aren't distinct realms, but rather interwoven parts of the same whole. They're intertwined, influencing each other continually.

Work-life integration does not imply working all the time. Instead, it's about fluidly shifting priorities based on immediate needs, sometimes giving more attention to work and other times focusing more on personal or family issues.

The core principle: flexibility

At the heart of work-life integration is the concept of flexibility. Sometimes work demands might necessitate long hours or encroach on personal time. At other times, personal or family matters might need more attention. Sometimes you may need to be focusing on work matters in the evenings, during traditional family time. And sometimes you may need to focus on family matters during your nine-to-five, traditional work time. The key is being able to flexibly shift focus between the two without feeling guilty or stressed and while still maintaining an overall balance in your life.

Reframing the way we perceive our work-life balance can lead to a more holistic and less stressful way of managing one's many responsibilities. By accepting the interconnectedness of our personal and professional lives and focusing on work-life integration, we allow for a more flexible and ultimately more sustainable way of living – a life where work and personal commitments coexist, rather than compete for our attention.

Practical steps for work-life integration

1. **Mindful prioritisation**: Acknowledge that at different times, different aspects of your life will take precedence. Be okay with allowing your focus to shift based on what's most important at any given moment. This requires an understanding that your priorities are dynamic, not static.

2. **Use technology, but smartly**: While it can tether you to work round the clock, technology can also provide the flexibility to work from anywhere, anytime. Use it to your advantage.

3. **Set boundaries**: Even though you are integrating work and personal life, it's still crucial to set boundaries to prevent burnout. These boundaries can be flexible, but they must exist.

4. **Communicate clearly**: Transparency with your team about your working style and expectations can prevent misunderstandings. Similarly, explaining your work commitments to your family can help them understand and support you.

5. **Self-care**: Taking care of your physical and mental health is crucial. Regular exercise, a healthy diet, and adequate rest can significantly improve your ability to cope with stress.

6. **Seek support**: Don't hesitate to seek help when you need it, both at work and at home. Delegate tasks, outsource if needed, and build a support network you can rely on.

The Delicate Balance Between Leading and Leaving

'It is better to lead from behind and to put others in front, especially when you celebrate victory when nice things occur. You take the front line when there is danger. Then people will appreciate your leadership.'

– Nelson Mandela

An effective leader understands the dynamic balance between leading and leaving – stepping forward to guide their team or stepping back to allow them to flourish. This delicate balance is what differentiates good leaders from great ones. While good leaders can drive a team to accomplish set goals, great leaders are skilled at empowering their team members, allowing for autonomy, creativity, and growth. And it's this knowledge

> Leaders guide by setting the direction, communicating the vision, defining roles, and supporting team members in their tasks.

that creates opportunities within your business for you *and* your team to flourish and strive towards achieving your 10% Differentiator.

Understanding the concept of leading and leaving

The 'lead or leave' balance in leadership refers to the delicate interplay between giving guidance and granting autonomy to team members. Leaders guide by setting the direction, communicating the vision, defining roles, and supporting team members in their tasks. However, when it comes to leaving, they allow team members the freedom to make decisions, learn from mistakes, and tap into their creativity.

This balance is crucial as it determines how team members perceive their leaders and how motivated they are to perform their roles. When leaders micromanage, they may stifle innovation and autonomy, leading to dissatisfaction and disengagement among team members. However, when they trust and empower their team, they foster a sense of ownership and pride in the work, enhancing performance and creativity.

Tools and mechanisms for effective leading and leaving

1. **Situational leadership**: This leadership model suggests that leaders need to adapt their leadership style based on the team's maturity level. In the early

stages of team formation, leaders need to provide more direction ('lead'). As the team matures and becomes more capable, leaders can shift towards a delegative style ('leave').

2. **Communication**: Leaders need to communicate clearly and effectively. They should clearly articulate their vision, goals, and expectations, and then encourage open dialogue to ensure team members understand their roles and responsibilities. When 'leaving', they should still maintain regular check-ins to offer support and feedback.

3. **Empowerment**: Leaders need to cultivate a culture of empowerment where team members feel trusted and valued. This can be achieved by delegating responsibilities, allowing decision-making autonomy, and supporting individual growth and development.

4. **Trust building**: Trust is a crucial element of the 'lead or leave' balance. Leaders need to demonstrate their trust in their team by granting them the freedom to perform their roles without unnecessary interference. However, this trust needs to be earned through competence, reliability, and integrity.

5. **Coaching and mentoring**: This is a key tool for leaders to guide their team members towards reaching their potential. Through coaching, leaders can help their team members acquire necessary skills and knowledge. 'Leaving' in this context could mean giving them real-world tasks to apply what they've learned.

6. **Feedback mechanism**: Leaders should establish a robust feedback mechanism for acknowledging successes, addressing mistakes, and guiding performance improvement. This helps maintain the balance as leaders can guide ('lead') their team through constructive feedback while fostering a sense of responsibility and accountability ('leave').

> The balance between leading and leaving is what sets great leaders apart.

The balance between leading and leaving is what sets great leaders apart. The best leaders know that leading isn't about having all the answers; it's about guiding their team towards finding their own solutions. By achieving the right balance, leaders can foster a culture of trust, autonomy, and innovation within their teams, driving high performance and growth. As a leader, always strive to answer the question: 'Do I know when to lead, and when to leave?'

'A leader is best when people barely know he exists, when his work is done, his aim fulfilled, they will say: we did it ourselves.'

– Lao Tzu

From Criticism to Constructive Growth: Embracing Feedback

'I think it's very important to have a feedback loop, where you're constantly thinking about what you've done and how you could be doing it better.'

– Elon Musk

One of the most challenging tasks for leaders is to find the right balance in terms of feedback. This means actively soliciting feedback and responding constructively to it whether positive or negative. Too often, a leader will welcome positive feedback but dismiss criticism, creating blind spots and limiting their growth potential.

To foster self-awareness, a fundamental trait of effective leadership, and to ultimately embrace your own 10% Differentiator, one must regard feedback not as a form of criticism, but as a powerful tool for personal and professional growth.

Understanding feedback

It's vital that we understand feedback – all feedback – because feedback acts as a mirror reflecting our actions and behaviours as perceived by others. It's important that we understand that feedback is inherently neither good nor bad but is simply information that can help affirm or reshape our actions.

While leaders might view compliments as affirmation and criticisms as indications of their shortcomings, it is crucial to understand that all feedback, whether positive or negative, presents an opportunity for growth (this is the balance we need to seek).

When leaders are open to feedback, they demonstrate a willingness to learn and adapt, which not only facilitates their personal growth but also encourages a culture of continuous learning within their team.

Creating your board of directors

A critical step to effective and balanced feedback is to carefully select who you ask for feedback. Just as companies have a board of directors to guide their strategic direction, leaders should have a group of trusted individuals who can provide them with objective and honest feedback. These people could be past colleagues, mentors, coaches, or friends who understand your professional aspirations and are willing to provide you with honest, constructive feedback.

When you ask for feedback from your board of directors, it's essential to keep an open mind. Don't dismiss their opinions if they challenge your views. Instead, ask for more details and seek to understand their perspective. The purpose of this exercise is not to defend your actions but to gain insights that will help you improve as a leader.

Responding to feedback

The ability to respond positively to feedback, irrespective of its nature, sets mature leaders apart. Acknowledging feedback with gratitude, whether it aligns with your self-perception or not, is critical in demonstrating your openness to learn and improve. It is also critical to ensuring that you continue to receive balanced information.

Resist the urge to justify or defend your actions and instead say, 'Thank you. Please tell me more.' This approach encourages further communication and fosters an environment in which feedback is welcomed and valued.

> Resist the urge to justify or defend your actions and instead say, 'Thank you. Please tell me more.'

Implementing feedback

Asking for and receiving feedback is just one part of the equation. Acting on that feedback effectively may prove to be even more important. Feedback is only valuable if it's put into action.

Once you've received feedback, reflect on what you've learned, assess its relevance, and determine the best course of action. It may involve developing new skills, altering behaviours, or reconsidering your approach to certain tasks. Feedback is a gift, an opportunity for self-improvement, a tool to guide your growth, and a catalyst for your evolution as a leader.

Building a culture of feedback

Embracing feedback as a leader has a positive ripple effect on your team. It fosters a culture of transparency, open communication, and continuous learning. By showing vulnerability in asking for balanced feedback and acting on it, you inspire your team members to do the same.

> Leadership isn't about perfection; it's about growth and continuous improvement.

Leadership isn't about perfection; it's about growth and continuous improvement. Feedback is a critical tool in this journey, enabling leaders to enhance their self-awareness, address blind spots, and constantly evolve. As a leader, invite feedback, accept it with grace, and use it as a stepping stone on your path to leadership excellence.

The 10% Differentiator in Action

Having balance in your personal and work lives, and in your approach to leadership, opens the door to growth. It opens the door to growing your abilities that next 10%, and taking your leadership to an exceptional level.

Here are some more real life examples of the 10% Differentiator in action.

Emotional maturity: lessons from coaching with Mohammed Aramany

'Coaching sessions hold a unique value. Many professional environments do not afford the time to delve into the emotional and functional issues inherent to each individual. Coaching provides an unparalleled focus on these areas. Key aspects included, improving communication skills, fostering realism, and managing emotions, all of which I've seen tremendous growth in myself since being coached.

Initially, I was entrenched in my own viewpoint, often preoccupied with my response rather than opening myself to new perspectives. This was a significant issue I struggled with, which has since been largely rectified. The shift may seem minor, but its impact on the business is profound, even if it's not readily quantifiable.

These in-depth discussions helped me explore areas needing enhancement, particularly regarding self-awareness. The one-on-one nature of these sessions ensured a comfortable environment where personal matters could be discussed without fear or hesitation. It's been a transformative experience.

Over the period of coaching, my understanding of my role has evolved. I initially thought it was 90% technical and 10% communication and personal development. Now, I see the balance as a more equitable 50/50 split. It's not just about dealing with work pressure, but also effectively engaging with managers, team members, and suppliers.

Coaching has equipped me with the essential skills needed for handling work-life balance, managing top management expectations, and comprehending various personalities. I was given a list of tasks to complete, and all the advice given to me was based on my position, business needs, and character. This personalised approach has been instrumental in my accepting and implementing changes without feeling they contradict my nature.

These sessions have indeed been transformative, not just professionally but also personally. I was struggling to balance family and work, and to engage properly with others. Now, I feel a significant difference even in the

> *way I listen to others' problems. This guidance has had a profound effect, and for that, I am truly grateful.'*
>
> **Mohammed Aramany – Marketing & Communications Director**

Key takeaways from Mohammed are:

1. **Improved communication**: Mohammed improved his communication skills and learned to understand others' perspectives rather than focusing solely on their response.

2. **Emotional intelligence**: He has grown in emotional intelligence, gaining a better understanding of his feelings and how to manage them, helping him to be more effective in his interpersonal relationships.

3. **Self-awareness**: Mohammed has enhanced his self-awareness, recognising personal areas of growth and change, helping him to become more adaptive and responsive.

4. **Leadership skills**: He has developed his leadership skills, learning how to deal with work pressure, engage effectively with managers, team members, and suppliers, and handle top management expectations.

5. **Work-life balance**: Mohammed has learned strategies by which to maintain a healthy work-life balance, an aspect he struggled with previously.

6. **Realism**: He has embraced realism, understanding that technical skills alone are not enough for success. He realised that interpersonal skills form a significant part of leadership roles, and is working towards balancing both.

Navigating the intricacies and complexities of a large corporate: lessons from coaching with Prashant Kamdar

'It is through my coaching sessions that I have been given the necessary guidance with which to navigate the intricate complexities and challenges that come with working in a large corporation. This clear and concise advice simplified what I initially perceived as substantial hurdles.

Coaching enabled me to understand the importance of prioritizing based on what matters to the relevant stakeholders, a perspective I had somewhat overlooked. Although I've always been aware of the importance of understanding people and believed in my communication skills, the emphasis on these aspects highlighted the need to continuously improve in these areas.

One crucial piece of advice that stood out was focusing on the individual in front of me, understanding their *needs and ensuring they feel heard and valued. Another was the guidance I was given regarding the prioritizing of tasks based on their urgency, impact, and ease of completion. This brought forth a lot of clarity. I appreciate how this approach has streamlined my thought process and improved my synergy with the team.*

These techniques were novel to me, but their implementation has considerably eased my professional journey. The time spent in coaching has enabled me to focus better on my work by bringing a new level of clarity. Consequently, this has promoted my professional growth - an impactful result of this coaching.'

Prashant Kamdar – CEO & Founder

Key takeaways from Prashant are:

1. The importance of **understanding and addressing the specific interests and needs of different stakeholders**. This understanding has made the process of navigating various business challenges more straightforward and less daunting.

2. Prashant has gained a heightened awareness of the significance of **interpersonal skills**, the importance of being **present and responsive** to individual needs, and of making each interaction **meaningful and constructive**.

3. Prashant has learned how to **prioritise tasks** based on their urgency, impact, and feasibility (therefore embracing the new work-life integration paradigm). This clarity has enhanced his decision-making abilities, facilitating a more efficient workflow.

Conclusion

While research shows us that balance is key in many ways, our own experience shows it as well. If you want to grow, if you want to achieve the incredible 10% Differentiator in your own work, you need to have balance in your work-life, in your leadership, and in the information that will assist you in your own growth. Of course, part of doing that well is understanding your values, and the shared values of your organisation and teams.

Values

Driving yourself and your team towards the 10% Differentiator requires many elements – but values are an important part. In fact, research shows that high-performing teams start with a culture of shared values.[11] As a leader, it becomes your job to be able to recognise where you and your team sit on the values spectrum, to ensure that you build the trust and connection that creates the opportunity for growth.

> Driving yourself and your team towards the 10% Differentiator requires many elements – but values are an important part.

You also need to ensure that you are prioritising your work – both your own, and that of your organisation as a whole – to align with those values. If you are able to do that, then you're in a key position to go from success to success and strength to strength, and truly embrace your next 10%.

Deconstructing Leadership and the Power of Alignment

'Understanding a person's hunger and responding to it is one of the most potent tools you'll ever discover for getting through to anyone you meet in business or your personal life.'

– Dr Mark Goulston, Psychiatrist

In our roles as leaders, we yearn for the autonomy to execute our vision, to drive change, and to cultivate a future we deem possible. Often, we find our paths obstructed by various stakeholders, each with their own unique expectations and directives. As we strive to do 'our thing', we often find resistance or even indifference at every turn.

This resistance often originates from a disconnect between ourselves and our team or other stakeholders. However, this disconnect arises because of a lack of shared understanding and values. So, it becomes clear that the secret to making strides toward our desired future – and our 10% Differentiator – lies in understanding, aligning, and expressing shared values.

During one of my coaching sessions with a seasoned managing director, he expressed frustration with the leadership style of his CEO. He shared, 'Regardless of my suggestions or actions, I constantly find myself at an impasse with my superior. It's as if he has no faith in my capabilities, making me question if I should even bother innovating.'

I probed further, asking if he could identify any recurring themes or values his CEO emphasised during their discussions and meetings. I explained, 'These recurring themes represent his core values. If you can align with and communicate in a manner resonating with these values, you'll likely find more acceptance and fewer barriers.'

I encouraged him to reflect on our conversation and share his insights via email. Later he told me, 'Referring to our recent one-on-one meeting, I would like to thank you a lot as it was a very fruitful discussion. Prior to our discussion, I was unaware of the root cause of the conflicts I've been experiencing in both my personal and professional life. Your insights have created a new perspective for me, emphasising the importance of being mindful of others' values.

Your guidance was spot-on, akin to "hitting the nail on the head". I hadn't fully grasped the significance of understanding others' values in various facets of life.

Here are some values I've observed in my supervisor:

- Family
- Success
- Honesty

- Friendship
- Public relations
- Respect
- Perfection
- Simplicity
- Precision
- Elegance
- To be a stand-out.'

By learning what mattered to his supervisor, my client was able to better understand and engage with him, and even become a better leader himself.

The importance of shared values

Shared values are the principles and standards that govern your company's actions. Because of that your shared values are vital in ensuring that every action you take is the right action.

When it comes to identifying values, every organisation will have a different set, conceptualised in a different way.

> Shared values are the principles and standards that govern your company's actions.

For example, Google's values are:

- Focus on the user and all else will follow
- It's best to do one thing really, really well
- Fast is better than slow
- Democracy on the web works
- You don't need to be at your desk to need an answer
- You can make money without doing evil
- There's always more information out there
- The need for information crosses all borders
- You can be serious without a suit
- Great just isn't good enough

By way of comparison, National Australia Bank lists their five core values as:

- Passion for customers
- Win together
- Be bold
- Respect for people
- Do the right thing[12]

The values of an organisation influence the decisions and actions taken by every individual and team within that organisation. These values, expressed by senior leaders, manifest as priorities (and, as such, factor into work prioritisation as well).

Aligning with expressed values

Once your shared values have been identified, the next step is to align actions and communications with these values. This alignment doesn't mean mimicking or parroting these values. Instead, it involves an authentic integration of these values into one's leadership style and decision-making processes. This is known as 'values-based leadership'.

How does values-based leadership look in practice? An example is that if a CEO emphasises speed, then this value should be reflected in the swift decision-making and execution of tasks. If accountability is a priority, the focus will be on creating a team that clearly understands their roles and responsibilities and holds themselves to high standards.

While core values are generally clearly expressed, leaders who want to rise from good to exceptional must hone their listening skills and cultivate a deeper understanding of the values expressed by their superiors or board members. By noting what is repeatedly emphasised, we can decipher these expressed values and begin to comprehend their significance.

Speaking the same values-based language as your stakeholders or superiors doesn't just enhance communication; it creates a connection based on mutual understanding and respect. This alignment is likely to foster trust – the bedrock of any successful relationship.

'If you talk to a man in a language he understands, that goes to his head. If you talk to him in his language, that goes to his heart.'

– Nelson Mandela

The trust dividend

Trust, once established, becomes a powerful catalyst. It opens doors that seemed previously locked and grants you the freedom and autonomy you desire and need. When stakeholders trust you, they are more likely to support your ideas and allow you the latitude to implement them. This then creates the opportunities for growth that will help you achieve your 10% Differentiator.

A practical exercise

An effective method with which to begin this alignment process involves jotting down the recurring themes, priorities, or concerns expressed by those in senior positions. You don't need to explicitly ask about their values; just listen carefully to their conversation, advice, or directives. Read between the lines to understand their underlying values.

Armed with this knowledge, you can begin to reflect these values in your own actions and communication. The alignment that you achieve can significantly bolster your career, improving your ability to enact meaningful change and bring your vision to fruition.

Navigating the waters of leadership can be challenging, but by aligning with shared values, building trust, and ultimately earning the freedom to lead effectively, you can turn these challenges into opportunities. Remember, understanding and aligning with shared values isn't a one-time effort, but a continuous process that can help you become a more effective leader.

> Understanding and aligning with shared values isn't a one-time effort, but a continuous process that can help you become a more effective leader.

Reading the Room

'The most dangerous person is the one who listens, thinks, and observes.'

– Bruce Lee

Just as we need to learn how to implement organisational values by observing other leaders, we also need to see how values are being understood by other members of our team or organisation. We can do this by learning to 'read the room'.

Reading the room, often termed as 'situational awareness', is an invaluable skill that can make or break a leader's success in both formal and informal environments. It is an intuitive understanding of the dynamics, emotions, and undercurrents within a group setting. It allows leaders to gauge the collective mood, anticipate reactions, and modulate their behaviour accordingly.

Understanding the concept of reading the room

Reading the room entails picking up and interpreting both explicit and implicit cues from the environment and the individuals present. These cues can be verbal or non-verbal, including tone of voice, body language, facial expressions, and even silence. It involves understanding the context, the interpersonal relationships at play, the unspoken rules of engagement, and the emotional temperature of the room.

'Knowing how to read between the lines is a critical workplace skill. You need to understand other people – what they want, what they don't want, their fears, hopes, dreams and motivations. This builds trust, and trust is fundamental to getting things done.'

– Annie McKee, senior fellow at the University of Pennsylvania and author of, *How to be Happy at Work.*[13]

Why is it crucial for leaders?

The ability to read a room is fundamental to effective leadership. It provides insight into team dynamics, aids in conflict resolution, and helps foster a supportive, collaborative atmosphere. Importantly it also helps leaders to see where values are being adopted and implemented, and where there might be gaps.

Leaders who can accurately read a room are able to empathise with their team, address underlying issues before they escalate, and align their communication style with the mood and needs of the group. Furthermore, this skill enhances values-based decision-making, negotiation, and persuasion capabilities, as leaders can tailor their approach based on the nuanced understanding of the situation.

How to develop 'room reading' skills

1. **Active listening**: The foundation of reading a room is to become an adept active listener. This involves fully concentrating, understanding, responding, and then remembering what is being said. Active listening helps decipher underlying messages, pick up subtle hints, and understand the unspoken concerns of the group.

2. **Observing non-verbal cues**: Non-verbal communication, including body language, facial expressions, and gestures, often reveals more than words. By being observant and understanding these cues, leaders can gain insights into the real sentiments behind the spoken words.

3. **Emotional intelligence**: This refers to the ability to recognise, understand, and manage both our own emotions and the emotions of others. High emotional intelligence allows leaders to sense the mood of the room, empathise with others, and adjust their communication accordingly.

4. **Consistency in behaviour**: Leaders need to be authentic and consistent in their behaviour. Inconsistencies can lead to confusion and mistrust among the team. Regardless of the situation, leaders

should strive to maintain their core demeanour and values.

5. **Knowing when to speak**: Reading the room also involves knowing the right moment to interject with comments or questions. This includes recognising when it's more effective to stay silent and let others lead the conversation.

6. **Self-awareness**: Leaders should be cognisant of their own influence on the room's atmosphere. They must understand how their own verbal and non-verbal cues might be interpreted by others, particularly when it comes to values.

7. **Adaptability**: Effective leaders are flexible and can adapt their communication style based on the situation. They can balance their need to be heard with the need to create space for others to speak.

Reading the room is a nuanced skill that every effective values-based leader needs to master. It involves listening more than speaking, understanding both verbal and non-verbal cues, and maintaining consistent and adaptive behaviour. Through conscious practise and continuous learning, leaders can cultivate this ability. This will enhance their leadership effectiveness, enable

> Reading the room is a nuanced skill that every effective values-based leader needs to master.

them to better implement organisational values throughout their team as a whole, and foster a more engaged and collaborative team environment.

If Everything is a Priority, Then Nothing is a Priority

'Time management is an oxymoron. Time is beyond our control, and the clock keeps ticking regardless of how we lead our lives. Priority management is the answer to maximizing the time we have.'

– John C. Maxwell

Discerning what truly requires immediate attention can be an overwhelming task. Leaders often find themselves in a quagmire of endless tasks, all seemingly carrying the same level of urgency and importance. This can result in leaders prioritising tasks that are easier to execute while postponing complex, even more critical, ones.

Understanding values-based prioritisation

Prioritisation is the process of arranging tasks or activities in order of their relative importance or urgency. Values-based prioritisation is the same process, but determining a task's importance or urgency is based on the values of an organisation.

Prioritising work requires strategic thinking and discernment, as leaders juggle multiple tasks demanding their attention. Often leaders end up prioritising the easiest tasks, while neglecting those that are complex but perhaps more impactful in the long run. This approach, while providing short-term relief, can lead to long-term repercussions.

Tools for prioritising tasks

Tool 1: The Eisenhower Matrix

Stephen Covey's four-quadrant matrix, also known as The Eisenhower Matrix, is an excellent tool for helping leaders prioritise tasks. It consists of four quadrants, categorising tasks based on their urgency and importance.

THE EISENHOWER MATRIX

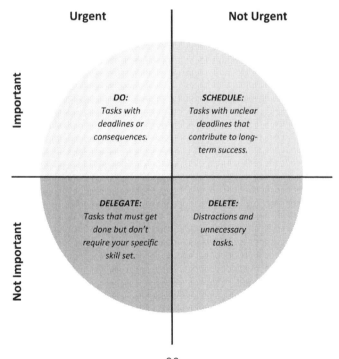

	Urgent	Not Urgent
Important	*DO:* Tasks with deadlines or consequences.	*SCHEDULE:* Tasks with unclear deadlines that contribute to long-term success.
Not Important	*DELEGATE:* Tasks that must get done but don't require your specific skill set.	*DELETE:* Distractions and unnecessary tasks.

Quadrant I includes urgent and important tasks, requiring immediate attention.

Quadrant II contains important but not urgent tasks – these are often strategic and contribute to long-term goals.

Quadrant III includes urgent but not important tasks that can typically be delegated.

Quadrant IV focuses on tasks that are neither urgent nor important and should generally be eliminated from the to-do list.

By understanding and implementing The Eisenhower Matrix, leaders can efficiently allocate their time and resources. This ensures that critical tasks are not neglected, and prevents burnout from focusing too heavily on urgent but less important tasks.

> By understanding and implementing The Eisenhower Matrix, leaders can efficiently allocate their time and resources.

Tool 2: The Value-Impact Matrix

The Value-Impact Matrix is another powerful tool for helping leaders prioritise tasks. This matrix is divided into four quadrants based on the ease of implementation and the impact on the organisation.

THE VALUE-IMPACT MATRIX

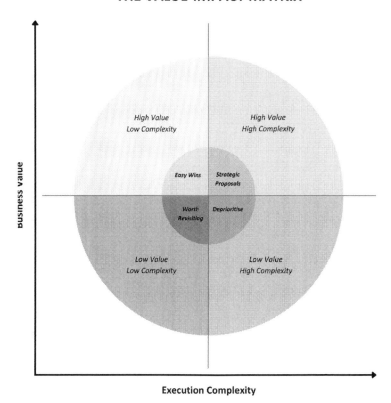

Quadrant I includes tasks that are easy to implement and have a high impact, which should be prioritized immediately.

Quadrant II contains high-impact tasks that are difficult to implement. These are often strategic initiatives that require careful planning and are implemented over a more extended period.

Quadrant III includes low-impact tasks that are easy to

implement and are not necessarily critical, but which can contribute to smooth day-to-day operations.

Quadrant IV includes tasks that are difficult to implement and have low impact—these should be avoided, as they consume significant resources with little return.

The Value-Impact Matrix encourages leaders to think strategically about their tasks, focusing on those that yield the greatest benefit for the organisation while also considering the resources required for implementation.

Integrating the tools for optimal prioritisation

By integrating both the Eisenhower and Value-Impact matrices, leaders can develop a comprehensive understanding of their tasks, assessing not only their urgency and importance but also their potential impact and ease of implementation.

To begin, leaders should map their tasks on the Eisenhower Matrix to identify those that need immediate attention, those that can be scheduled for later, those that can be delegated, and those that should be eliminated. Next, the tasks in the first three categories should be evaluated on the Value-Impact Matrix. This will allow leaders to assess the potential return on investment for each task, taking into consideration the effort required for their implementation.

These assessments should always be undertaken with an overarching focus on the shared values of the organisation. When this is done well, then the dual-matrix approach to prioritisation provides a clear roadmap for leaders, enabling them to make informed, values-based decisions about task allocation and execution.

Perhaps the easiest way to explain this process is to consider how we deal with our emails on a daily basis. Many leaders fall into the trap of coming into the office, and immediately starting with their emails. If we are honest with ourselves, we would recognise this is a task that does not take much effort or brainpower. Yet, we can spend quite a bit of time on this task. In my experience, not a lot of the emails we receive are critical or urgent. They might all have some level of importance – but how impactful are they *really* at this time? Aren't there tasks that could better use a fresh mind and an urgent focus? If so, what are those tasks?

Once we start thinking about our tasks in this way it changes our perspective. The questions we need to ask are:

- Is this important?
- If so, is this urgent?
- Is it easy to resolve, and does the resolution have high impact?

Over time our thinking changes and we automatically give priority to the most urgent and most impactful tasks, as opposed to those tasks that might be easy to do, but which aren't urgent and / or have little impact.

By distinguishing between what is urgent and what is important, and understanding the potential value and impact of their tasks, leaders can manage their time more effectively, reduce stress, and ultimately, drive their organisation towards success.

The 10% Differentiator in Action

Values-based decision-making allows leaders to take action and grab opportunities for growth so that the next 10% becomes easily achievable.

How Richard Crawley uses self-reflection as a values-based decision-making process

'Particularly in the motor industry, leadership positions often attract a specific type of individual. In such a setting, we can tend to limit ourselves within the confines of established norms. Therefore, engaging in coaching sessions is crucial to pushing our boundaries, testing our capabilities, and challenging our self-perceptions.

Progressively, my aspiration is to step out of my comfort zone, boosting my self-belief. Unless I foster this belief within myself, I cannot convincingly inspire my team. My goal is to evolve as a leader, thereby adding value not only to my team but also to my peers. It is essential to expand my emotional capabilities in leadership rather than solely focusing on the operational aspect.

Reflecting on my development, I have gained greater self-confidence and belief in my professional and personal capabilities. This progress encourages me to regularly pause and evaluate my daily achievements and shortcomings, particularly in the evenings. I assess the team's performance and its implications on our business productivity. This exercise equips me with a unique skill set for addressing business challenges.

This coaching journey has provided me with insights on handling people, be it my peers or my subordinates.

From a personal standpoint, it has significantly bolstered my self-belief. I now set aside a brief period each day for self-reflection and even jot down the positives. It's an exercise in recognizing and focusing on the positives rather than being caught up in the negatives. This practice has helped me to sideline unproductive thoughts and people and to concentrate on our accomplishments.'

Richard Crawley – MD Specialist Repairs

Key takeaways from Richard are:

1. He recognised the importance of **stepping outside his comfort zone** and challenging his self-perceptions to evolve and grow as a leader.

2. Richard discovered that **self-belief and confidence** are not only essential for personal development, but also crucial for inspiring and leading his team effectively.

3. He learned the value of **introspection**. He found that by taking a moment each day to pause and reflect on his achievements, challenges, and the team's performance, he was provided with valuable insights. This helped him develop a unique skill set with which to tackle business challenges and manage his interpersonal relationships better.

It is all about maintaining that personal connection: lessons from coaching with Romi Chugh

'In my experience, I've come to realize that while it's crucial to maintain a professional demeanour, it's equally beneficial to humanize our interactions in the workplace. Recognizing that personal connection can be instrumental in driving motivation and productivity, is an understanding I've developed over time.

This coaching has assisted in bringing my latent potential to the forefront, in an articulate and straightforward manner. From the start in October till now, I've been cognizant of what needs to be achieved. However, the guidance I have got from the coaching sessions, has provided me with effective strategies with which to accomplish my goals in a manner that is not only efficient but also more suitable for my style of working. Establishing priorities, identifying opportunities, and *focusing on factors that engender joy for others have all become clearer thanks to these sessions.*

Emphasizing the 'Good to Great' philosophy, I acknowledge that while we may not be at the pinnacle of greatness, we're certainly on a progressive path towards becoming better versions of ourselves.

One key learning that I've incorporated is the importance of flexibility and understanding in interactions. It's become evident that productivity stems from a collaborative process infused with a certain level of authority. Communicating in a language that resonates with the individual has been a lesson well learned. I've understood the importance of building relationships even when it's not directly related to an immediate task, which has proven to be extremely beneficial for accomplishing goals.

Trust, I've learned, is built on the foundation of effective communication and relationship building. As we understand more about our peers' preferences, they start to identify with us on a more personal level leading to increased cooperation. Understanding their preferred modes of communication helped streamline our interactions, making the process simpler and more efficient. This is a testament to the fact that resolving minor challenges can lead to significant improvements in productivity.'

Romi Chugh – Director and Co-founder

Key takeaways from Romi are:

1. He realises the value of fostering **personal connections** in a professional setting. This interpersonal knowledge can increase motivation and work output.

2. Romi has discovered his own **potential** and that of his team. The coaching process has illuminated ways to effectively tap into and utilise this potential.

3. The importance of **balancing collaboration and authority** has become clear to him. Work efficiency can be boosted while respecting each team member's individuality.

4. He recognises the value of **relationship building beyond immediate work needs**. This includes understanding individual likes, dislikes, and values which can be instrumental in fostering **trust** within the team.

5. He has learned to appreciate **the impact of minor changes**. Even small adjustments can lead to significant improvements.

Conclusion

To embrace high performance and productivity – in other words, to move yourself and your team from good to great – you need to understand and develop shared values within your organisation. A culture of shared values ensures you'll be able to make values-based decisions and build the trust and connection that creates the opportunity for growing into your full potential.

Potential

Tapping into your individual potential, as well as your overarching organisational potential, can be the step you need to move from good to great, and from great to exceptional. To elevate your potential, you need to be able to elevate your productivity, taking it from an overwhelming whirl to a targeted force for growth. While there may be issues that can hold you back, there are steps to overcome these as well.

Tapping into your individual potential, as well as your overarching organisational potential, can be the step you need to move from good to great, and from great to exceptional.

Your Productivity Peak: Reshape Your Day for Success

'Success is the product of daily habits – not once-in-a-lifetime transformations.'

– James Clear

In the dynamic environment of leadership, there's a constant whirl of tasks, responsibilities, and priorities that need managing. Leaders often grapple with where to begin and end, resulting in strategic and future-focused tasks taking a back seat to the pressing urgencies of the present. It is, therefore, vital to introspect, identify, and harness our most productive hours in a day to create impactful change and harness our real potential.

Understanding individual productivity peaks

Productivity peaks are those specific periods during a day when individuals find themselves most energised, creative, and efficient. This differs among individuals – some are at their best early in the morning, while others in the afternoon or evening.

The first step towards harnessing this productivity peak is recognising when it occurs. Reflect on when you feel the most energised, inspired, and capable of complex thought. Pay attention to patterns in your mood, energy, and productivity over several days or weeks. By identifying these patterns, you can pinpoint your productivity peak.

Harnessing your peak for strategic tasks

Once you've identified your most productive time, the next step is to align it with your most demanding tasks. These are typically strategic tasks requiring creativity and complex thought – the tasks that shape your future. If you've noticed that your peak productivity occurs early in the morning, schedule your strategic tasks during this time.

> Once you've identified your most productive time, the next step is to align it with your most demanding tasks.

All too often, overwhelmed by a multitude of tasks, leaders start their day with easier tasks like responding to emails. While this might seem efficient, it consumes the time when they could be the most productive, leading to a missed opportunity for strategic thinking and planning. Match your peak productivity periods with your most demanding tasks to maximise your efficiency and elevate your potential.

Utilising off-peak periods for routine tasks

Just as there are peak productivity periods, there are also off-peak periods when your energy levels dip. Identify these periods and allocate routine tasks, which do not require a lot of cognitive effort, to these times. This could include tasks like email management, administrative work, or routine meetings. These tasks, while necessary, don't necessarily drive strategic growth, making them perfect for off-peak times.

This approach ensures that your productivity peaks are dedicated to high-impact, strategic tasks, while routine tasks are taken care of during your off-peak periods.

Implementing tools for effective time management for managing productivity

A strategic approach to managing your productivity peaks and off-peak periods can revolutionise your work efficiency. This is important because when you are more productive, you've tapped into your potential, and are able to reach more of your 10% Differentiator.

There are several tools and techniques you can use to support this approach:

1. **Time blocking**: This technique involves blocking out specific times in your calendar for different types of tasks. Use it to set aside your peak productivity periods for strategic tasks and your off-peak periods for routine tasks. This ensures your high-energy times are dedicated to high-impact tasks.

2. **Prioritisation matrix**: This helps sort tasks based on

their urgency and importance. You can use it to identify which tasks to tackle during your productivity peak and which to handle during your off-peak periods. (See Eisenhower Matrix, Chapter 4)

3. **Digital tools**: Several apps and digital tools can help manage your time effectively. These include task management apps, project management software, and productivity trackers. Use them to plan, organise, and track your tasks based on your productivity peaks and off-peak periods.

Rethinking team productivity

Just as you have productivity peaks, so do your team members. Encourage them to identify and harness their productivity peaks to increase their own individual potential, and your team potential as a whole. This can boost overall team productivity and morale.

You might want to consider flexible work schedules to enable team members to work during their peak productivity periods. Or you may want to think about workflow systems that will help your team prioritise their own tasks to their own productivity peaks.

Regardless of the tools or systems you implement, take the time to reflect on the effectiveness of your approach regularly. Are you getting more done during your productivity peak? Is your team? Is this helping each to reach their potential? Regular reflection will help you refine this approach.

Potential for transformation

Embracing your productivity peak is a transformative step. It allows you to move beyond merely dealing with the present to shaping the future. With strategic time management, you can make your productivity peak work for you, transforming your potential.

Breaking Free: Overcoming Self-Limiting Beliefs to Unleash Your Potential

'Remember you have been criticising yourself for years and it hasn't worked. Try approving of yourself and see what happens.'

– Louise Hay

From constraints to catalysts: overcoming self-limiting beliefs

Many of us have experienced moments when we've held back, hesitated, or shied away from certain actions or conversations we know we need to have. This could be a necessary sales conversation or a difficult conversation with team members, or even approaching a superior about remuneration. It could be embracing the systems we need to become more productive.

Despite being crucial, we often postpone or avoid these conversations or actions. This avoidance keeps us from performing at our best and from reaching our full potential.

The role of self-limiting beliefs

Our resistance to taking action can stem from our own thought patterns. We tell ourselves we're not smart enough, not good enough, or that our intended approach might not be correct.

In neuropsychology, these thought patterns are recognised as **self-limiting beliefs** – they limit us from our full potential.[14] These self-limiting beliefs originate from past experiences and over time, they get so deeply ingrained that we start believing them, even when they aren't true. Even seasoned leaders can have these beliefs in some shape or form.[15]

'If you raise your standards but don't really believe you can meet them, you've already sabotaged yourself. You won't even try; you'll be lacking the sense of certainty that allows you to tap the deepest capacity that's within you ... Our beliefs are like unquestioned commands, telling us how things are, what's possible and impossible and what we can and can not do. They shape every action, every thought and every feeling that we experience. As a result, changing our belief systems is central to making any real and lasting change in our lives.'

– Tony Robbins

How do we navigate these self-limiting beliefs?

1. First, when these limiting thoughts arise, **acknowledge** them. Identify them for what they are and give them a name. Recognise the avoidance, understand the fear, and label it as a self-limiting belief. For example, you might say, 'I don't want to have this sales conversation because I don't think I'm good enough.' Or 'I can't talk to my boss about this because I don't believe it's the right way.'

2. Second, once identified, the next step is to **reframe** these beliefs. Byron Katie, a speaker and author, offers a powerful way to reframe negative thoughts. She suggests asking yourself, 'Is this thought really true?'[16] Your initial response might be affirmative, but upon repeating the question, you might start to question the belief. By asking, 'How would I feel without this thought?' you recognise that without this belief, you might be free.

Understanding the shackles of the mind: defining self-limiting beliefs

When we embark on the journey of leadership, we often find ourselves at a crossroads where our ambitions meet our self-perceived limitations. These mental barriers (or self-limiting beliefs) are negative assumptions that curtail our potential, dampen our confidence, and keep us from setting and achieving meaningful goals. They are like invisible chains, keeping us tethered to our comfort zones and inhibiting progress. 'I'm not smart enough,' 'I'm not cut out for this,' 'I'll never be successful,' or 'I'm just not good enough' are just a few examples of the self-limiting beliefs that many of us carry.

Origins: where do self-limiting beliefs come from?

The science behind self-limiting beliefs resides at the intersection of psychology and neuroscience. Self-limiting beliefs are largely born from our past experiences, societal and cultural conditioning, childhood impressions, and habitual negative self-talk, which shape our self-perception, and guide our thoughts, emotions, and behaviours.[17] The brain tends to reinforce these beliefs through repeated thought patterns, which can consolidate these negative ideas, making them seem like unshakeable truths.

These beliefs often form as a coping mechanism, a kind of mental armour that shields us from anticipated failure, rejection, or criticism. This armour, however, is a double-edged sword. While it can offer a false sense of security, it also imposes invisible boundaries on our capabilities, thus hindering our growth and potential.

A catalogue of constraints: common self-limiting beliefs

Although self-limiting beliefs are unique to everyone, some common themes emerge. These often manifest as feelings of inadequacy, anticipated failure, undeserving success, or inherent lack of ability. Beliefs such as 'I'm not good enough,' 'I'm not smart enough,' 'I'll never be successful,' 'I can't do this,' and 'I don't deserve success,' are examples of the internal barriers many of us face.

The leadership link: the impact of self-limiting beliefs on leadership development

In the realm of leadership, these self-limiting beliefs can have a profound impact. They can restrict a leader's potential and negatively influence their team's dynamics and performance. Overcoming these self-imposed limitations can lead to substantial growth both on an individual and team level – particularly important when you're striving to meet your 10% Differentiator.[18]

This metamorphosis can result in increased self-confidence, improved decision-making abilities, enhanced communication skills, heightened motivation, more effective team management, and increased resilience. Changing self-limiting beliefs can thus unlock the leader's true potential and drastically improve their effectiveness.[19]

Path to empowerment: a 7-step process to overcome self-limiting beliefs

Overcoming self-limiting beliefs is not a quick fix, but a continuous journey of self-discovery, reflection, and personal growth. It involves seven core steps:

1. **Identify the belief**: Begin by acknowledging and precisely articulating the self-limiting belief. Write it down and own it.

2. **Explore the origin**: Dive into the past and try to locate where this belief might have originated. This could be a remark from someone in the past or a negative experience that shaped this belief.

3. **Evaluate the evidence**: Objectively examine the supporting and contradicting evidence for this belief. Recognise instances where this belief was proven false.

4. **Reframe the belief**: Based on the evidence gathered, reinterpret the belief. Replace the negative belief with a positive one that aligns with your capabilities and aspirations.

5. **Practise self-affirmations**: Regularly engage in positive self-talk and affirmations that reinforce the new, positive belief.

6. **Visualise success**: Create a mental picture of yourself acting in accordance with the new belief. Imagine your actions, reactions, and overall success with this new perspective.

7. **Take action**: Put the new belief into action. Start taking small but consistent steps towards your goals in line with the new belief.

Once we've acknowledged and reframed these self-limiting beliefs, it's time to take action. Begin taking small steps towards confronting these issues, even if you feel uncomfortable or underprepared. Test your limits, challenge your beliefs, and you'll soon see that the more you practise overcoming these barriers, the easier it becomes, and eventually, it starts feeling natural.

This process requires time, patience, and a consistent willingness to reflect, learn, and grow. It is not a one-time solution but an ongoing effort to challenge and transform self-limiting beliefs. Small steps towards change taken today will lead to significant personal and professional growth in the future.

> Many leaders grapple with a common self-limiting belief: the fear of public speaking.

Many leaders grapple with a common self-limiting belief: the fear of public speaking. Although public speaking is an integral aspect of leadership, it can evoke overwhelming anxiety in some. Here's an example of a structured approach to navigate and potentially overcome this belief.

1. **Identify the belief**: 'I'm not proficient at public speaking and might embarrass myself.'

2. **Explore the origin**: This belief could have roots in an early setback, like stumbling over words during a presentation or facing unexpected laughter from an audience.

3. **Evaluate the evidence**: Upon introspection, you might recall:

   - Successfully delivering a speech at an event and being complimented.
   - Earning top remarks for a presentation during training or educational endeavours.
   - Contributing ideas in team meetings that were well-received and appreciated.

4. **Reframe the belief**: 'While I've faced challenges with public speaking, I've also experienced successes. Through diligent preparation and practise, I can enhance my abilities.'

5. **Practise self-affirmations**: Consistently remind yourself, 'I have the potential and capacity to be an impactful public speaker. Every opportunity to speak is a chance to hone my skills.'

6. **Visualise success**: Envision confidently addressing an audience, observing their engagement, and receiving positive feedback.

7. **Take action**: Seek out speaking engagements, prepare

with care, and engage with confidence, reinforcing the new, empowering belief.

As a very young graduate trainee in a highly demanding automotive manufacturing facility, I was often challenged on many levels. There were many times even when I doubted my own abilities and was very unsure about my own capabilities. I shall never forget my human resources manager, Adrian Nel, who on one occasion said to me, 'Anton, there is absolutely nothing in HR that you cannot do.' This belief in my skills as a young HR professional would set the tone for the rest of my life. His absolute belief in me totally outweighed any self-limiting beliefs I may have had. I have so much to thank him for.

Just as I experienced personally, acknowledging, reframing, and acting against self-limiting beliefs can unleash potential and improve performance. The first step is to recognise these self-imposed barriers, then challenge them by reframing our thoughts and perceptions, and finally, to take the leap and act, despite any lingering self-doubt. Overcoming self-limiting beliefs isn't easy, but the freedom and growth on the other side make the journey worthwhile.

Addressing potential blind spots

A blind spot is a behaviour or characteristic you are not aware of but is obvious to others. The Johari window, developed by Joseph Luft and Harry Ingham in 1955, is a useful psychological model that gives individuals an enhanced understanding of themselves and how are they perceived by others.[20]

THE JOHARI WINDOW

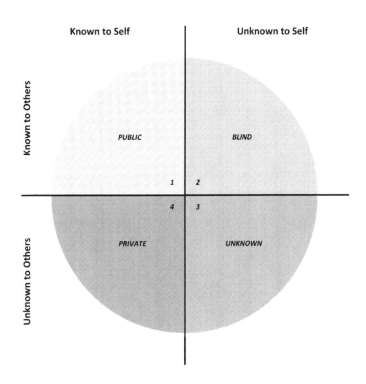

The model is comprised of four quadrants, or 'window panes', that signify thoughts, feelings and motivation, and whether this information is known or unknown to the self. In essence, it uncovers your blind spots, which can highlight a weakness that is unknown to you. This weakness could become a block to your growth and development.

One way to identify a blind spot is through a 360-degree leadership behaviour process. A 360-degree leadership review, also known as 360-degree feedback or multi-rater feedback, is a system in which employees receive confidential, anonymous feedback from the people who work around them. This typically includes the employee's manager, peers, and direct reports.

Amongst other outcomes the 360-degree leadership review process uncovers blind spots in one's performance by gathering feedback from various sources. This comprehensive approach includes perspectives from peers, subordinates, and superiors. Comparing this feedback to an individual's self-assessment highlights discrepancies, which are often indicative of blind spots. The process's anonymity promotes candid feedback, and consistent patterns from different sources solidify the identified areas for improvement. In essence, this multi-faceted feedback acts as a mirror, reflecting behaviours and actions that the individual might not be aware of, helping them grow personally and professionally.

Over-Indexing and Under-Indexing

When we're working on adopting leadership principles, we have to be aware of the potential of over-indexing and under-indexing. Both can lead to an imbalanced leader which will decrease your potential and high performance, rather than achieving your goal of increasing growth and influence.

> Over-indexing is where a leader puts too much effort and focus on one or two parts of their leadership or values.

Over-indexing is where a leader puts too much effort and focus on one or two parts of their leadership or values. For example, this could be 'Deep dive.' A leader who is over-indexing may spend so much time on this that they fail to focus on other values, such as 'Earn trust' or 'Customer care.' Those values that have lost focus will then become under-indexed, and in this example, your customer relationships will falter even where your expertise thrives.

Having this imbalance in leadership stops other members of the team from taking initiative in these areas, and demonstrating their own passion and innovation. In addition, having this narrow-minded focus can undermine the long-term growth and productivity of your team and organisation. Instead, we need to seek balance in our leadership principles in order to ensure that we're gaining in productivity and become a more efficient, high-performing team.

The 10% Differentiator in Action

Going from good to great and from great to exceptional means tapping into your potential. And in order to achieve your potential you'll need to elevate your productivity by addressing your blind spots and overcoming the things that hold you back.

The results from making these changes can be immense, including helping you to increase your successes at work and achieve your 10% Differentiator.

Implementing personal and professional development to drive your trajectory: lessons from coaching with Sanjeev Aggarwal

Sanjeev Aggarwal says his trajectory in his organisation would have been so different if he had been unable to implement personal and professional development.

'I was privileged to participate in this executive coaching program, which commenced in December 2020. The initiation of this program began with an assessment by an expert, followed by a session discussing our strengths, weaknesses, and areas of improvement. This gave us a robust understanding of our individual capabilities and offered a structured roadmap for personal and professional development.

Reflecting on the past two years, I can assertively state that the trajectory of my progression within the organisation would have been dramatically different without these coaching sessions. The structured approach and thought-provoking questions in every session stimulated personal evolution and growth, a remarkable benefit of the program.

Moreover, transitioning into a new country, with an unfamiliar culture and business structure, presented its own set of challenges. However, the program served as a platform where I could share these concerns within my professional network. The combination of structured and unstructured sessions, coupled with my coach's patient and attentive listening, aided me significantly in overcoming perceived obstacles and accelerated my pace of adaptation.

Following each session, I experienced noticeable improvement in my reactions and responses to various situations. Almost every piece of advice provided proved beneficial, aiding me in navigating through complex circumstances.

Indeed, reaching a position of leadership entails ticking numerous boxes, such as qualification, experience, and business expertise. Yet, my coach's focus on addressing potential blind spots and stretching my capacities further was truly insightful. He approached even the most challenging subjects delicately, ensuring that feedback was framed as an opportunity for growth rather than a complaint. This approach transformed my perspective and increased my receptiveness to feedback.

The sessions aimed to bring to light those 10% areas that may be our blind spots or opportunities. My coach's ability to empathize, to step into my shoes during discussions, significantly improved my acceptance and understanding of the issues at hand. It helped me perceive feedback not as a complaint, but as an opportunity to better myself.'

Sanjeev Aggarwal – Director of Operations

Key takeaways from Sanjeev are:

1. **Increased self-awareness**: Due to the expert assessment, Sanjeev gained a deeper understanding of his strengths, weaknesses, and areas that required improvement.

2. **Adaptability**: The coaching sessions equipped him with the skills needed to navigate through a new cultural and business environment, enhancing his ability to adapt in unfamiliar circumstances.

3. **Emotional intelligence**: Sanjeev learned to recognise and overcome perceived obstacles that he had mentally created, enhancing his emotional intelligence.

4. **Receptiveness to feedback**: His coach's approach encouraged him to see feedback as an opportunity for growth rather than as a complaint, fostering greater openness to critique.

5. **Empathy**: Sanjeev developed an improved understanding of how to put himself in others' shoes during discussions, leading to more effective communication and problem-solving.

Embracing your 10% to instigate profound change: lessons from coaching with Samir Kozem

'I must assert that the seemingly small 10% impact from these coaching sessions has indeed instigated a profound change, influencing my entire personality and overall approach.

The perspective shift brought about by these sessions has enriched my understanding, sharpened my analytical ability, and shaped my responses to various situations. In essence, it has revolutionized my leadership style and managerial approach, augmenting my effectiveness within the workplace.

To illustrate, as I transitioned into a more senior role, I was increasingly affected by feedback from my subordinates, colleagues, and upper management. This often distracted me and negatively impacted my performance. These coaching sessions elucidated the situation, guiding me on how to insulate my performance from extraneous influences. As I began to comprehend the impact of these distractions, I redirected my focus towards my tasks, fostering a more serious and respected professional persona.

Moving forward, I believe it's crucial to continue this coaching journey. I advocate for not only senior leadership but also middle-management professionals aspiring for leadership roles to receive focused coaching. This guidance will aid them in refining their behaviour and leadership style. Once they transition into senior roles, they would benefit from expert coaching with which to enhance their leadership capabilities further. The ultimate aim is to create a more conducive workplace and to foster personal growth.'

Samir Kozem – GM Sales

Key takeaways from Samir are:

1. **The 10% adjustment** has had a holistic impact on his potential, affecting his entire personality and the way he views both work and personal matters.

2. The coaching sessions have provided him with **insight** into how others perceive his actions and reactions, which has been integral to his personal and professional growth.

3. Samir has learned how to better handle pressure that comes with a senior role and how not to let **feedback** distract from his focus on performance.

4. The coaching helped him realise the **impact of external influences** on his performance, enabling him to concentrate more on his tasks.

Mastering leadership is an art rooted in over-indexing on unique strengths: lessons from coaching with Kalyana Sivagnanam

'When it comes to core leadership capabilities, such as IQ, EQ, job-specific knowledge, and domain expertise, I see them as foundational, or what I'd term 'hygiene factors'. Possessing these skills sets the stage for your journey in leadership, but they don't guarantee sustained success.

I often compare this to learning a language, specifically English. A novice starts with the alphabet, progresses to grammar, and then delves into literary giants like Shakespeare to expand their vocabulary. But an extensive vocabulary alone doesn't make one eloquent. That person has grasped the science of the language but remains unfamiliar with the nuanced art of communicating effectively. I draw a parallel here with leadership. These foundational skills (IQ, EQ, and the like) are the scientific aspect; the art comes in when you know how and where to over-index these skills, applying them effectively in diverse scenarios.

This brings us to the "10%" you mentioned, a differentiator. Every individual will over-index differently based on their strengths. For instance, one CEO might be over-indexing on their astute business insights, while another might be renowned for their exceptional people skills. Each leader, in essence, over-indexes in a domain that sets them distinctly apart from the rest.

A pertinent example is the cohort of students from renowned institutions embark on the same educational journey, yet only few emerge as CEOs. This discrepancy isn't about the foundational skills – all of them possess that. It's about how and where they are over-indexed. It's this act of over-indexing, be it in hard work, perseverance, emotional resilience, or business acumen, that creates the defining line.

It would be an oversimplification to concretely define this "10%" or encapsulate it within a formula. Every individual's 10% varies. As leaders, recognizing our areas where we can over-index, harnessing them while concurrently being aware of our shortcomings, and proactively seeking assistance or resources for improvement, is pivotal.

Reflecting on my own journey, I've always been acutely aware of my strengths and more importantly, my shortcomings. I've never been under the illusion that mastery in several domains equates to effective leadership. In areas I felt deficient, I've actively sought external assistance rather than attempting to self-correct. I've always had clarity on what I excel at and have consistently pushed those strengths to the forefront. This introspection and self-awareness have been instrumental in my successes. It's not about being the best in every domain but recognizing where you shine and optimizing that.

In closing, your concept of the "10%" is not about quantifying leadership; it's about understanding where one's strengths lie, where they can over-index to truly make a mark. This awareness and the journey of harnessing it have been instrumental in my leadership path.'

Kalyana Sivagnanam – Group CEO

Key takeaways from Kalyana are:

1. **Leadership fundamentals**: IQ, EQ, job knowledge, and specialised expertise are foundational elements in leadership, termed as 'hygiene factors'.

2. **Learning analogy**: Mastering leadership is similar to learning a language. While one can learn the basics (the 'science'), true eloquence or effectiveness (the 'art') comes from deeper understanding and practise.

3. **The 10% Differentiator**: Beyond foundational skills, there's a unique 10% that sets apart great leaders. It's the element where an individual significantly over-indexes or outperforms.

4. **Prestigious Institution example**: While many start with the same foundational skills, as evidenced by students at prestigious institutions, only a select few rise to the topmost leadership roles. This distinction is often due to where they choose to over-index.

5. **Personal reflection**: It's essential for leaders to be introspective, recognising their strengths and areas of over-indexing, while seeking external help for their weaknesses.

6. **Over-indexing**: Effective leaders don't aim to be the best in every domain. Instead, they identify their unique strengths and amplify those, making them stand out.

7. **Holistic view**: Leadership isn't just about mastering the fundamentals. It's about identifying and leveraging one's unique strengths to make a meaningful impact.

Conclusion

If you're striving to achieve your 10% Differentiator, you will need to tap into your own full potential and capabilities. In the same way, organisations must tap into the full potential and capabilities of their employees to thrive. To do this, both as an individual and an organisation, involves elevating productivity and ensuring that you don't succumb to self-limiting beliefs or traps that might hold you back.

Doing this, however, will set you up to see you as you truly are, in all your potential. Once you can do that, it's time to step up your leadership skills.

Leadership

Of all the 10% Differentiator elements covered in this book, leadership might seem the most obviously applicable. After all, many of those reading this are likely leaders or emerging leaders looking to grow and expand their own influence. It's how we grow and expand as leaders that matters.

> Many of those reading this are likely leaders or emerging leaders looking to grow and expand their own influence.

To achieve growth that really allows you to embrace the potential found in the 10% Differentiator requires you to focus on developing your leadership, starting with what you can influence and what you can't. Learning how to feel and express empathy and when to let your team take the lead are other factors to take stock of. Each of these will help when working on elevating your own leadership from good to great.

Control and Influence in Leadership

*'I cannot always control what
goes on outside. But I can always
control what goes on inside.'*

– Wayne Dyer

Leadership, much like life, revolves around managing uncertainties, dealing with frustrations, and steering through environments where control can sometimes seem elusive. As leaders, we might find ourselves entangled in challenges, which, while pressing, are beyond our immediate sphere of control.

This realisation can trigger feelings of frustration and even incapacitation. However, recognising what is within our control and harnessing our ability to influence those things can alleviate this angst and enhance our leadership effectiveness.

Identifying the source of frustration

In coaching sessions, leaders frequently express frustration over a perceived lack of traction or progress. The sources of their angst are typically external: other people's actions, words, and even the general economic environment. However, dwelling on elements outside their control can be an exercise in futility and a drain on productivity.

So, how does one navigate this tricky terrain? The first step is identifying and distinguishing between what we can and cannot control.

Distinguishing between control and influence

Control in leadership is the capacity to directly change circumstances or behaviours in our environment. This extends to our actions, decisions, and interactions.

Influence refers to the ability to sway or shape situations, behaviours, or decisions indirectly.

Although we might not have full control, we can guide or contribute to the outcome through our influence.

Exercise to differentiate between control and influence

1. On a sheet of paper, create two columns.
2. In the first column, list all the things causing frustration that are outside your control. This might include the economic environment, actions of peers or superiors, or external factors affecting your team's performance.
3. In the second column, list things within your control: your actions, words, decisions, strategies, and the way you communicate with and manage your team.

Reflecting on these lists provides a fresh perspective on where your energy and focus should lie, and allows you to focus on the right things – the things you can control and influence.

EXERCISE TO DIFFERENTIATE BETWEEN CONTROL AND INFLUENCE

Shifting focus to control and influence

Spending time worrying about things outside our control is a waste of time. Conversely, focusing on what we can control empowers us to take decisive action, shape our environment, and drive tangible change.

For example, you may not be able to control the economic

climate, but you can control your strategic response to it. You can adjust your plans, reallocate resources, and develop new initiatives to adapt to and thrive in this new environment. Likewise, you may not control what your colleagues say or do, but you can control your reactions, the way you communicate, and the way you manage your team.

> Spending time worrying about things outside our control is a waste of time. Conversely, focusing on what we can control empowers us to take decisive action, shape our environment, and drive tangible change.

Beyond our direct control lies the sphere of influence, where we may not have outright control, but we can still make an impact. For instance, we can influence team morale through our leadership style, even if we can't control each individual's emotions. Similarly, we may be able to influence decisions at higher levels by effectively communicating our insights, even if the final decision is not ours to make.

Expanding control through influence

The interplay between control and influence is critical. The more we exercise control over areas within our direct reach, the more influence we can exert over areas just outside that sphere.

This expands our reach, creating a ripple effect that extends our leadership impact even further.

Leaders who focus on their controllable realm find themselves able to effect more substantial changes in their teams and organisations. Their proactive stance also boosts their influence, helping them shape even those aspects that were once outside their control.

This doesn't mean that we'll be able to control everything. However, it does mean we can expand our influence, mitigate frustration, and increase effectiveness.

'Be a light, not a judge, be a model not a critic. Little by little, your circle of influence will explode, and you will avoid the emotional metastasizing cancers of complaining, criticizing, competing, comparing and cynicism, all which reflect victimization, all of which are the opposite of being proactive.'

– Stephen Covey

The Power of Empathy in Leadership

*'In a high-IQ job pool, soft
skills like discipline, drive,
and empathy mark those who
emerge as outstanding.'*

– Daniel Goleman

The core of leadership lies in connecting with people, inspiring creativity, fostering innovation, and facilitating performance. All these things we yearn to achieve as leaders hinge on one fundamental ability: practicing empathy.

> As leaders, we often think about what it is that will elevate us from being a good leader to a great one.

As leaders, we often think about what it is that will elevate us from being a good leader to a great one. Empathy emerges as a crucial differentiator.

Empathy vs sympathy

Sympathy refers to feeling sorrow for someone else's situation – a form of emotional understanding that can sometimes make us feel better but does little to help the other person.

Empathy is about listening, asking questions, and truly understanding what someone else is going through.

While both are valuable, research shows that leadership empathy is vital for excellent outcomes, leading to higher levels of innovation and engagement, better retention, more inclusivity, and a more balanced work-life.[21]

The practise of empathy in leadership

The practise of empathy in leadership doesn't always come naturally. As leaders, we may find ourselves preoccupied with action items, deadlines, and strategic priorities, leaving little time for introspection, or understanding the nuances of our team members' lives. However, this understanding – the comprehension of what they are thinking, saying, doing, and feeling – is crucial for establishing genuine connections.

The power of connection

Our goal as leaders is to foster creativity, drive innovation, and motivate our team members to deliver exceptional results. These outcomes will remain elusive if we fail to create an environment

> Our goal as leaders is to foster creativity, drive innovation, and motivate our team members to deliver exceptional results.

where employees feel they belong, where they believe their leaders genuinely care about them.

Without this sense of connection and care, employees may clock in and out, delivering what's required but withholding the creativity, passion, and dedication that truly elevate performance. The practise of empathy allows us to resolve this disconnect, cultivating an environment where employees feel understood, appreciated, and valued.

> *'Empathy is a strange and powerful thing There is no script. There is no right way or wrong way to do it. It's simply listening, holding space, withholding judgment, emotionally connecting, and communicating that incredibly healing message of "You're not alone".'*
>
> – Brené Brown

The practise of empathy

Practising empathy in leadership involves more than mere lip service. It requires asking genuine questions about our team members' lives – their thoughts, feelings, and experiences. It requires us to be present, engaged, and invested in their responses. It necessitates prioritising people over processes and understanding over task completion. With empathy comes connection and a sense of belonging amongst our team members, which ultimately leads to improved performance.

The more we practise empathy, the more natural it becomes. While challenging at first, empathy becomes second nature with persistence. And the results – improved connection, greater employee engagement, enhanced performance – make this practice not only beneficial but essential for any leader.

To transition from a good leader to a great one, we must listen, understand, and connect genuinely with our team members. It may require a shift in focus and approach, but the rewards make it a pursuit worth the effort.

Shifting Lenses: Embracing Diverse Perspectives

'If there is any one secret of success, it lies in the ability to get the other person's point of view and see things from that person's angle as well as from your own.'

– Henry Ford

Leaders need to recognise the power of diverse perspectives in problem-solving. Every individual within a team brings a unique perspective, influenced by their experiences, skills, and knowledge. By inviting and valuing these different viewpoints, leaders can drive innovation, improve decision-making, and foster a more inclusive culture.

> Every individual within a team brings a unique perspective, influenced by their experiences, skills, and knowledge.

Incorporating multiple perspectives allows leaders to:

1. Approach problems from **various angles**.
2. Foster **innovative solutions** that wouldn't be possible with a single perspective.

3. Ensure a **broader understanding** of issues which helps **anticipate potential challenges**, and leads to more **holistic and effective solutions**.

4. Cultivates a **sense of belonging** among team members, reinforcing the notion that their thoughts and opinions matter, thereby **improving team morale and productivity**.

Broadening your leadership perspective: a pathway to inclusivity

Given the potential benefits of incorporating diverse perspectives, how can leaders adjust their approach to avoid the pitfalls of a single-minded perspective?

The answer lies in developing active listening skills and fostering a culture of open communication.

To gain alternative viewpoints, leaders need to create an environment where others feel comfortable expressing their thoughts and ideas. This starts by leaders demonstrating that they value and respect different perspectives. It involves asking open-ended questions that stimulate discussion, and actively listening to the responses. Leaders should resist the urge to interject with their thoughts, instead encouraging others to share their ideas freely.

Cultivating a culture of open dialogue: a step-by-step guide

1. **Self-awareness**: Begin by acknowledging the influence of your personal perspective on your leadership style and decision-making process. Understand that while your viewpoint is valid, it is not the only one, and other perspectives may offer valuable insights.

2. **Foster open communication**: Create a safe space for team members to express their ideas and opinions without fear of judgement or retribution. Encourage open discussions, and ensure all voices are heard.

3. **Active listening**: Practise active listening, paying full attention to the speaker, and avoiding interruptions. Reflect on what's being said and respond thoughtfully.

4. **Ask open-ended questions**: Instead of leading with your perspective, ask open-ended questions that encourage others to share their thoughts and ideas. This allows you to gain insights you may not have considered otherwise.

5. **Promote diverse viewpoints**: Foster a culture that values diversity of thought. Encourage team members to share their unique perspectives and experiences.

> Foster a culture that values diversity of thought.

6. **Respect differences**: Understand that disagreements and debates are healthy and a natural outcome of diverse viewpoints. Ensure these discussions remain respectful and constructive.

7. **Implement feedback**: Show your team that their input matters by implementing their feedback when feasible. If an idea isn't used, provide clear reasoning why, demonstrating respect for their contribution.

8. **Continual learning**: Regularly reassess your communication style, seeking feedback from your team, and adjusting your approach as necessary. Remember, developing a broad perspective is a journey, not a destination.

By following this guide, leaders can begin to broaden their perspective, creating a more inclusive and effective leadership style that drives innovation and fosters a healthy team dynamic.

'Good leadership requires you to surround yourself with people of diverse perspectives who can disagree with you without fear of retaliation.'

– Doris Kearns Goodwin

Lead From the Front or Lead From Behind

'The world is changed by your example, not by your opinion.'

– Paulo Coehlo

As we talked about in Chapter 3, leadership is a complex dance of sometimes taking the helm and sometimes stepping back to empower others. Both styles have their strengths, applicability, and unique effects on a team's dynamics and performance. Learning how to balance and shift between them is the mark of an exceptional leader.

Leading from the front: visibility and accountability

Leading from the front signifies a visible, hands-on leadership approach. These leaders are often the face of the team, making strategic decisions, setting goals, defining behaviours, and taking responsibility for the team's successes and failures even when others don't want to. A great example is Malala Yousafzai, a young woman who, despite facing Taliban oppression in Pakistan, spoke out against injustices in her community. Her leadership from the front (in fact, where almost no one had ventured before) inspired a generation of others and led to her winning a Nobel Peace Prize.

Leading from the front is about clarity in communication and expectation. These leaders articulate their vision, define roles and responsibilities, and set clear deliverables. They hold team members accountable for their work, fostering a sense of responsibility and commitment within the team.

However, leading from the front is not just about enforcing rules or taking charge. These leaders also actively model the behaviours and values they expect from their team members, creating a powerful example that can shape the team's culture and work ethic.

Leading from behind: empowerment and humility

While the concept of leading from the front might be more familiar, the art of leading from behind is just as important. Leading from behind is about enabling others to shine, promoting shared leadership, and fostering individual and team growth.

In South African President Nelson Mandela's autobiography, *Long Walk to Freedom*, he talks about leading from behind. He says that great leaders oversee their people like a shepherd tends their flock of sheep. And just like the shepherd remains behind the flock, the leader stands behind their team, encouraging and guiding but letting the most passionate and innovative in the group set a path for the rest.

Behind-the-scenes leaders are those who empower their team members to take the initiative, make decisions, and deliver results, recognising where others will shine. They provide guidance and support when needed, but their primary focus is on developing their team's capabilities and independence.

Leading from behind means promoting others' success, even if it means staying in the background. These leaders understand their success lies in the success of their team members and other stakeholders. This approach requires humility, self-awareness, and a keen understanding of the dynamics of influence and power.

Striking the balance

1. **Understand the team's needs**: Teams go through different stages of development and will require different leadership styles at different times. A newly formed team might need more directive, frontline leadership, while a mature, high-performing team could benefit more from behind-the-scenes leadership.

2. **Practise emotional intelligence**: Reading the room and understanding your team's emotions and needs can help you decide when to lead from the front or from behind. Emotional intelligence is key to being flexible and responsive to the situation at hand.

3. **Develop trust**: Trust is the cornerstone of both forms of leadership. Building trust with your team allows you to lead effectively from the front, while also giving you

146

the confidence to step back and let your team take the reins when appropriate.

4. **Encourage shared leadership**: Great leaders know they don't have to do it all. They encourage team members to take leadership roles in areas where they excel, creating a more collaborative and empowering environment.

5. **Manage your ego**: Leading from behind often requires you to put your ego aside and let others shine. This doesn't mean that you're not contributing; it means you're contributing to a collective success, which can be highly rewarding.

'Great CEOs have an "everyone wins" mentality, and their leadership style is about developing everyone to do their best. They cannot be all ego. They must have a vision and strategic direction ability, but the ones I have seen that do the best, engender the best in everyone around them.'

– Janet Zaretsky, The Zenith Business[22]

A good leader knows when to take charge and when to step back.

A good leader knows when to take charge and when to step back – when to lead from the front and when to lead from behind. It's a balance that takes practise, self-awareness, and an unwavering commitment to your team's success. Effective leadership is not about personal glory but about guiding your team to reach their full potential. In doing so, leaders create an environment where everyone can thrive – leading to collective success and fulfillment.

The 10% Differentiator in Action

Excellent leadership can mean the difference between seeing you reach your full potential (as well as your team) and struggling in the shallows. Effectively implementing the differentiators – such as an empathetic perspective, and identifying and clearing sources of leadership friction – leads to excellent leadership in practice and is how you create change and growth that matters.

The importance of an empathetic perspective: lessons from coaching with Tariq Javed

'Without a doubt, these sessions over the past year have been quite enlightening. Every conversation has offered me new insights or an additional perspective that has enriched my understanding and approach to various situations, projects, roles, or engagements with business and people. While stepping into a new role brings its unique challenges, some that we expedite for the very first time. It's our skills, capabilities and personal traits built over years that usually guide us through these new experiences, however, not all challenges can be resolved through past experience. And that's where these conversations have been notably beneficial.

Having access to another's viewpoint has allowed me to perceive things through a different lens, to approach *situations with a renewed perspective. I can confidently say that each interaction has been fruitful, leaving me with useful insights that have significantly enhanced my ability to manage specific scenarios.*

This guidance and support throughout the program has been invaluable. It's been instrumental in my personal growth and progression as a leader, aiding me in navigating through new experiences and challenges effectively.'

Tariq Javed – CEO Automotive

Key takeaways from Tariq are:

1. **Enhanced understanding**: Tariq learned that every conversation and interaction could offer new insights, enriching his approach to various situations, projects, roles, and engagements.

2. **Perspective broadening**: He quickly grasped the value of viewing things from different, empathetic lenses, realising that not all challenges could be addressed solely based on past experiences.

3. **Value of external input**: Tariq appreciated the usefulness of insights from a different viewpoint, understanding that it could significantly improve his approach to managing specific scenarios.

Identifying sources of frustration in leadership: lessons from coaching with Terence Byrne

'In articulating the value of these coaching sessions, I would say this: as one ascends the ranks in an organisation, a certain level of isolation can set in. Many times, we find ourselves relying heavily on instinct and past experiences, which can be beneficial to a point. However, what I've found enlightening about these sessions is the fresh perspective they bring to various challenges, conversations, and circumstances.

As a senior leader, it can be easy to become rigid or one-dimensional in our thinking. Moreover, we may often encounter situations where individuals offer affirmations rather than honest feedback. The coaching sessions have proven invaluable in presenting different viewpoints and unveiling potential insights previously unconsidered, thereby providing a distinct advantage.

Moreover, these sessions serve as a consistent, monthly opportunity for frank, candid, and transparent discussion about the challenges I face. The judgement-free space allows for open contemplation about potential perceived shortcomings, fostering a constructive environment for growth.

> In essence, these sessions encourage self-reflection, acting as a mirror where I can critically assess my responses to various situations. Amidst the daily hustle, carving out time for this kind of introspection is critical. It helps to evaluate our approach to the challenges presented and contemplate potential improvements.'
>
> **Terence Byrne – CEO Automotive**

Key takeaways from Terence are:

1. **The importance of different perspectives**: The coaching sessions helped Terence realise that considering diverse viewpoints is vital for comprehensive problem-solving and decision-making.

2. **The benefit of identifying sources of frustration**: Coaching gave Terence the space to consider his own frustrations around perceived shortcomings, so he could create a constructive environment for growth.

3. **The value of honest feedback**: He found that genuine, constructive criticism often yields more value than simply hearing what one might want to hear.

4. **The power of self-reflection**: Regular introspection has allowed Terence to critically evaluate his responses to various situations and identify potential areas for improvement.

Management vs empathetic leadership: lessons from coaching with Tony Mazzone

'From a business perspective, my personal management style has been shaped by a combination of life experiences, learned values, and previous professional encounters. Through these collaborative discussions, I've gained the ability to step back and critically evaluate why I manage the way I do.

A key revelation has been the distinct difference between management and leadership, as well as their respective values. Particularly, the insights regarding empathy have been invaluable, especially as I navigate a new culture and country.

Previously, my management approach yielded successful outcomes. However, achieving success in this new environment requires a different style. This guidance has provided me with the necessary tools to reassess and adapt my management approach to achieve optimal results.

From a team dynamics perspective, there was a crucial need to develop a structured overview. We had previously underestimated the essential process of storming, forming, and performing for a new team. The expectation was instant performance, overlooking *the need for this natural progression. The workshop illuminated certain areas needing support but lacked the knowledge to address. It provided us with a robust structure that could be applied to improve our overall team effectiveness.*

From a leadership standpoint, receiving honest 360-degree feedback was enlightening, clarifying the next steps necessary for team growth and improvement. The workshop has not only provided clarity about our performance level but also furnished a roadmap to elevate our performance. This structured approach has been extremely beneficial for my leadership role.'

Tony Mazzone – Director EV Infrastructure

Key takeaways from Tony are:

1. **The clear distinction between management and leadership**: Tony learned that these two concepts, although often used interchangeably, have different values, and require different skill sets.

2. **The importance of empathy in leadership**: In a new cultural environment, empathy becomes a crucial skill in understanding, communicating with, and managing a team.

3. **The necessity of adapting management style**: Success in different environments and cultures may

require different management approaches. Tony has learned to reassess his traditional style to achieve optimal results in his new context.

4. **Understanding team dynamics**: Tony has gained insight into the natural progression of team development – storming, forming, and performing. This knowledge helps to set more realistic expectations for team performance.

5. **The value of feedback**: Receiving honest 360-degree feedback from the team helped Tony identify areas for improvement and clarified his next steps.

Conclusion

Learning how to take your leadership from good to great is a significant part of leaning into the elements that drive your own 10% Differentiator. When it comes to elevating your leadership, simply start with learning where to best focus your energies, embracing empathy in your leadership styles and applications, and then using this to help understand when you need to lead from the front and when you're better to guide from behind.

When you lead like this you open yourself, your team, and your organisation to exponential growth that will lead to embracing your full potential and stepping into your influence.

Influence

The ability to influence is an essential leadership skill. When you are able to influence others, you impact their behaviours, attitudes, values, and even actions. This is not about having control or manipulating others to get your way. It's about listening and engaging with others to see what motivates them to achieve better outcomes for all.

When you have influence you are able to create more opportunities that align with your values and commitments. This will then lead to greater potential for exponential growth. However, to

> When you have influence you are able to create more opportunities that align with your values and commitments.

have influence you have to take steps to become an influential leader. This includes being coachable yourself, coaching others well, and learning how to inspire with storytelling.

Being Coachable: Embracing Humility and Growth

'Yesterday I was clever, so I wanted
to change the world. Today I am
wise, so I am changing myself.'

– Rumi

In coaching conversations, we often come across individuals who seem to know everything. No matter what advice we offer, they respond with statements like, 'Yes, I know, I've done that.' Or, 'I understand all of that.' Engaging in such conversations becomes challenging because it is clear that no one can possibly know everything.

While extreme cases of this behaviour can be particularly difficult to address, the tendency to believe we know it all, to some extent, is prevalent in most of us. This resistance to external input can hinder our growth and prevent us from truly listening and implementing valuable advice. However, by cultivating humility and embracing a coachable mindset, we can create an environment conducive to personal and professional development that will allow us to strive for our greater potential.

Recognising the limits of our knowledge

It is crucial to acknowledge that no single individual possesses all-encompassing knowledge, and that includes ourselves. Even leaders or experts in a particular field have their limitations. When we assume we know everything, we close ourselves off to new perspectives, alternative solutions, and invaluable insights. This mindset impedes our growth and prevents us from reaching our full potential.

The role of ego in hindering growth

One of the primary reasons for our reluctance to listen and accept advice is our ego. Our ego fuels the belief that we are always right and that others have nothing substantial to offer. Ego-driven individuals tend to prioritise their own voice, dismissing the wisdom and experiences of others.

Ego also creates a barrier that obstructs our ability to learn and grow. Consequently, we remain trapped within our comfort zones, missing out on valuable opportunities for personal and professional advancement.

Finally, an inflated ego makes us susceptible to manipulation, narrows the field of vision, and can cause us to act against our values, limiting our ability to influence others well through our leadership. Altogether, ego erodes leadership.[23]

Developing humility and openness

Breaking free of an inflated ego is an important and challenging job. To overcome the limitations posed by our ego, we must cultivate humility and openness. Humility allows us to recognise and embrace our limitations, making room for new knowledge and perspectives. By acknowledging that there is always more to learn, we open ourselves up to the possibilities of growth and development.

> To overcome the limitations posed by our ego, we must cultivate humility and openness.

Practical tools for developing humility

- **Active listening**: Instead of focusing solely on our own voice, we should strive to understand and empathise with others. Actively listening to different viewpoints fosters a deeper appreciation for the value of diverse perspectives and enhances our capacity for growth.

- **Acknowledging when we don't know something**: Instead of pretending to have all the answers, we should be comfortable admitting our lack of knowledge. This admission opens doors for further exploration, inquiry, and learning. By asking questions and seeking clarification, we demonstrate our willingness to expand our understanding.

- **Implementing valuable advice**: Being coachable goes beyond listening and recognising our limitations — it involves putting into practice the advice and knowledge we acquire. To effectively implement valuable advice, we must adopt a growth-oriented mindset and embrace a willingness to change:

1. Approach advice with an **open mind**. Rather than dismissing suggestions outright, take the time to carefully evaluate their potential benefits. Even if an idea seems unfamiliar or challenges your existing beliefs, consider the possibility that it may lead to growth and positive outcomes.

2. Setting aside our ego allows us to accept constructive criticism and feedback. **Constructive criticism** is an opportunity for growth, as it highlights areas for improvement and helps us identify blind spots. By embracing feedback, we can refine our skills and continuously enhance our performance.

The power of being coachable

A CEO from a prominent global automotive company, headquartered in a foreign country, faced a leadership crisis. He was responsible for a vast array of divisions, from manufacturing to human resources. However, despite his impressive resume and expertise, the results under his leadership were stagnant. The root of the problem? A vast cultural difference between him and his host country, leading to misunderstandings and reduced accountability.

As he worked in his role, his frustrations mounted. 'In my

country, when a task is given, it's executed. Why am I constantly double-checking here?' However, his employees viewed him as distant, believing he neither cared about them nor understood their culture. Their sentiment – 'He's just another expat who will leave soon.'

The CEO, realising he needed guidance, approached me. As his mentor and coach, I advised that true leadership isn't just about directives but understanding and connection. 'To truly lead,' I told him, 'you need to immerse in their culture. They need to see you as one of them. Your actions, words, and demeanour – how you are perceived – will determine if they follow.'

This showed the CEO that he had a problem with self-awareness. As his mentor, I highlighted his approach to leadership, demonstrating that while his approach was potentially effective in his home country, it simply wasn't suitable here. The CEO learned the significance of being coachable: openness to feedback, a willingness to adapt, and recognising that some traditional methods might not work in every setting.

Choosing growth over resistance, the CEO embarked on a journey of self-improvement and cultural immersion. He prioritised understanding his employees' motivations, values, and aspirations. The change was evident. The CEO's newfound approach sparked enthusiasm throughout the company. Hierarchical directives evolved into influential leadership. Measurable results, from profits to employee satisfaction, soared.

However, change often meets resistance. Some employees, preferring the old structure where they could shirk responsibilities, couldn't adapt. But as they left, aspirational talents came in, drawn by the company's rejuvenated culture.

Ultimately, the business thrived. Market share increased, employee morale skyrocketed, and the company's reputation became a beacon in the industry. The once-criticised CEO now had a team willing to go the extra mile for him and the organisation.

Being coachable is a sign of strength

At the end of the day, being coachable isn't a sign of weakness but a strength, especially for leaders. Being coachable is a mindset that requires us to shed our ego, embrace humility, and actively seek personal and professional growth. Recognising that we don't know everything and being open to learning from others' experiences expands our knowledge and perspectives. Active listening, asking questions, and admitting when we don't know are powerful tools for nurturing humility. By embracing feedback, understanding diverse perspectives, and adapting accordingly, leaders – such as the CEO above – can harness their team's full potential and pave the way for shared success.

Throughout my tenure as an Executive Coach, I am frequently posed a recurring question by those I coach: 'Where do you derive your satisfaction or reward from, especially when the outcomes of your efforts aren't visibly quantifiable?' It's a valid question. Unlike certain professions where success is easily measurable through distinct metrics, my fulfillment is more abstract yet nonetheless profound. It emanates from witnessing the transformative change and personal growth in the individuals I guide. As time progresses, these subtle shifts culminate into substantial differences.

However, it's imperative to note that such evolution is contingent upon the executive's receptiveness and genuine willingness to embrace and enact change – as such, being coachable.

By implementing valuable advice and accepting constructive criticism we facilitate our continuous improvement and development. By cultivating a coachable mindset, we unlock opportunities for growth, enhance our decision-making capabilities, and position ourselves for success in various aspects of life. Let us strive to be open, receptive, and eager to learn, for it is in our willingness to grow that we discover the true extent of our potential.

> By implementing valuable advice and accepting constructive criticism we facilitate our continuous improvement and development.

The Leader as a Coach: Harnessing the Power of Engagement Through Coaching Conversations

*'No matter what people
tell you, words and ideas
can change the world.'*

– Robin Williams

Why Leader-Coaches?

The competitive and dynamic nature of today's corporate landscape necessitates a transformation in the approach towards leadership. No longer can leaders afford to remain mere managers; they must evolve into efficient and effective coaches. High-performing leaders have come to understand that the key to unlocking performance lies in the frequency and quality of conversations they have with their team members. They appreciate the value of each interaction, viewing every meeting as a golden opportunity to coach and inspire their employees.

This approach challenges the traditional 'management by remote control' mentality. Instead, these innovative leaders prioritise getting to know their team members on a personal and professional level. They create space for discussions that not only boost performance but also foster genuine, enduring relationships.

Gallup's research substantiates the need for such an evolution in leadership, highlighting that employees seek purpose and meaning in their work.[24] They yearn for recognition of their unique attributes and capabilities. Perhaps most significantly, they crave a nurturing relationship with a manager who can coach and guide them towards the next level in their careers.

All of this leads us to understand that a direct supervisor can influence an employee's engagement by an incredible amount. In fact, as the studies show, they can influence engagement by an impressive 70%.[25]

Four engagement areas

Leaders must strive for excellence in four crucial areas of engagement:

1. **Performance and an engaged culture**: As leader-coaches, we must cultivate an environment that not only encourages exceptional performance but also nurtures a culture of engagement. This involves acknowledging good work, providing constructive feedback, and creating an atmosphere conducive to open communication and collaboration.

2. **Transitioning to an agile and innovative culture**: We must champion an agile work culture that embraces change and encourages innovation. This involves breaking down bureaucratic hurdles, encouraging out-

of-the-box thinking, and enabling teams to respond swiftly to changing market dynamics.

3. **Addressing fairness and inclusion**: Leader-coaches must foster an environment that celebrates diversity, champions fairness, and promotes inclusion. This involves acknowledging and valuing the diverse backgrounds, perspectives, and talents within the team, and ensuring that every team member has an equal opportunity to thrive and grow.

4. **Retaining young talent among older generations**: With multiple generations co-existing in the workplace, leader-coaches must strike a balance between leveraging the wisdom and experience of older generations and harnessing the fresh perspectives and tech-savviness of younger talent.

We become like the leaders before us

Leaders wield tremendous influence in shaping the behaviours, beliefs, and habits of their team members. As Sir John Whitmore aptly put it, 'Unlocking a person's potential to maximize their own performance is about helping them to learn rather than teaching them.'

This statement underscores the significant role a leader plays in developing their team. It's a reminder that the act of coaching transcends the traditional employer-employee dynamic, transforming it into a relationship centred around mutual growth and development.

However, leader-coaches must also recognise and acknowledge their fallibility. The journey to becoming an effective coach is a continuous process of learning and unlearning. We must confront and overcome certain obstacles that hinder us from being effective coaches.

Why we fail as coaches

Leader-coaches might stumble in their coaching journey for several reasons:

1. **Perceived softness**: Some leaders view coaching as a 'soft' approach to enhance performance. They believe that driving performance through authority and control is more effective than coaching. However, new leadership models recognise the fallibility of command-and-control leadership.[26] Instead, coaching leadership creates an environment of trust and respect that fosters greater long-term engagement and productivity.

2. **Leader confidence**: Overconfidence can be a significant impediment to effective coaching. Leaders who believe they have all the answers tend to instruct rather than coach, missing out on the rich insights that can emerge from a coaching conversation.

3. **Urgency**: The hustle and bustle of the corporate world often create a sense of urgency. Leaders may feel that providing instructions expedites task completion, whereas coaching takes more time. However, coaching

builds capacity and capability, empowering team members to solve problems independently and effectively.

4. **Lack of preparation**: Coaching requires specific skills that must be learned and honed over time. Leaders who dive into coaching without proper training or preparation may struggle to coach effectively.

Becoming a leader-coach matters

Transitioning to a leader-coach role offers a myriad of benefits:

1. **Promotes self-leadership**: As a leader-coach, you foster an environment of self-leadership. This not only enhances your own skills but also empowers your team members to take ownership of their tasks and responsibilities.

2. **Hones listening skills**: Coaching necessitates active and empathetic listening, which enables you to understand your team members' perspectives better, build empathy and respond more thoughtfully.

3. **Cultivates a culture of accountability**: When you coach your team members, you help them identify solutions to their problems, which encourages them to take responsibility for their actions.

4. **Fosters a high-performance culture**: Coaching conversations can illuminate the path to better

performance by identifying strengths, weaknesses, and opportunities for growth.

Formal and Informal coaching conversations

There are a myriad of coaching conversations we can have with our employees. However they can be broadly divided into two categories – formal and informal.

Formal coaching conversations are standard. They're the performance reviews based on KPIs and structured development discussions. While these are significant, they shouldn't overshadow the value of informal conversations.

Informal coaching conversations take place on two levels:

1. The first is at the **workstation**, where employees spend the bulk of their time. These casual yet critical discussions can shed light on ongoing issues, potential obstacles, and the general pulse of the team.

2. The second is the underappreciated practice of **one-on-ones**. Many leaders mistakenly view one-on-ones as mere opportunities to run through a to-do list, focusing on tasks to be accomplished and progress updates. However, these sessions should be perceived as an empathetic exchange where the emphasis is on the individual and not the tasks at hand. Questions should probe the individual's thoughts, feelings, concerns, and aspirations. It's an opportunity to

better understand their world, both professionally and personally.

These conversations should centre around their issues, their worries, even if they're not strictly work-related. A one-on-one, after all, is not just a check-in. It's a coaching session – a platform for growth, understanding, and connection.

Coaching conversations can be grouped into four distinct categories

1. **Formal reviews**: These discussions are centred around KPIs, progress, projects, and opportunities. They provide a structured platform for feedback and performance enhancement.

2. **Formal development**: These conversations focus on competency development, cross-functional projects, and individual development plans. They enable leaders to identify and nurture the potential within each team member.

3. **Formal check-ins**: Regular one-on-one meetings scheduled at set times provide a consistent platform for addressing ongoing issues and discussing growth opportunities.

4. **Informal check-ins**: Casual interactions at workstations, on-site, or off-site offer invaluable opportunities for coaching. They provide insights into

the pulse of the team, uncovering potential issues and identifying ways to improve the work environment.

The coach's mindset

A coach's mindset is critical for leaders as it promotes individual growth and self-reliance, enhances problem-solving skills, and fosters stronger team relationships. Furthermore, it contributes to cultivating a positive work culture that encourages continuous learning, feedback, and innovation. Adopting a coach's mindset is an effective strategy for boosting team performance and overall organisational success.

An effective coach embodies a distinctive mindset

1. **Growth**: Coaches encourage development and provide opportunities for growth. They help team members set challenging yet achievable goals and support them in their journey towards these goals.

2. **Meaning**: Coaches ensure that work is meaningful by discussing its purpose and significance. They help team members understand how their individual roles contribute to the larger organisational goals.

3. **Curiosity**: Coaches maintain a sense of curiosity. They ask thought-provoking questions, listen actively, offer alternative perspectives, and challenge the status quo.

4. **Optimism**: Coaches inspire hope and optimism.

They celebrate successes, instil confidence during challenging times, and keep the team focused on the future.

5. **Empathy**: Coaches empathise with their team members. They strive to understand their thoughts, feelings, and needs, demonstrating genuine interest and concern for their wellbeing.

The coaching conversation result

Coaching conversations allow leaders to foster improved productivity, leadership effectiveness, and employee self-efficacy.[27] By addressing individual needs, creating personal development plans, and encouraging a solution-oriented approach, leaders can facilitate career progression, cultivate a more engaged workforce and boost potential.

> Effective coaching conversations equip leaders with a more adaptive, higher-performing, and continuously evolving team.

Effective coaching conversations equip leaders with a more adaptive, higher-performing, and continuously evolving team. The open communication environment nurtures stronger, more authentic relationships, creating a more closely-knit team. These conversations can also aid in succession planning by identifying and nurturing future leaders.

An effective coaching conversation should lead to:

1. **Learning**: A reflection on what went well, what could have been better, and what lessons can be gleaned for future improvement.

2. **Insights**: The revelation of new knowledge or perspectives that were previously unknown or unexplored.

3. **Next steps**: The establishment of clear actions to be taken, responsibilities to be assigned, and plans for follow-up, ensuring the momentum from the coaching conversation carries forward.

The 4-step coaching conversation

The coaching conversation follows a structured, four-step process:

1. **Coaching content**: Begin by discussing the coaching content, which involves setting the agenda and ensuring both parties are aligned on the conversation's purpose.

2. **Coaching conversation**: Next, engage in the actual coaching conversation, which involves exploring ideas, providing feedback, and discussing opportunities for development.

3. **Coaching conclusion**: Summarise the key points discussed, reach an agreement on the next steps, and schedule a follow-up meeting to review progress.

4. **Coaching check-in**: Finally, carry out a check-in after the conversation, where you assess progress, provide further feedback, and adjust plans as needed.

The Leader as a Coach

Coaching for Success

The 4-Step Coaching Conversation

STEP 1. COACHING CONTENT

(List the name of the person, subject, business matter, behaviour, improvement, reward etc. up for discussion).

STEP 2. COACHING CONVERSATION

Formal Performance Review *(Review KPI's, objectives, milestones, projects etc.)*

Formal Development Review *(Review development opportunities, training requirements, competencies, individual development plan etc.)*

Formal Check-in *(Regular 1:1's, feedback-meetings etc.)*

Informal Check-in *(At desk, walk-by, off-site, canteen etc.)*

STEP 3. COACHING MINDSET

Curious *(Ask, listen, test status quo, question)*

Optimistic *(Provide hope, aspirational future, possibilities, a new way)*

Empathy *(Question; what are they thinking, feeling, saying, doing – needs and insights?)*

Meaningful *(Provide purpose and meaning, reasons, the why, what is in it for them?)*

Growth *(Provide development opportunities, stretch assignments, cross functional projects)*

STEP 4. COACHING RESULT

Insights: *What do I know now that I had not known before? Any other insights?*

Next Steps: *Action steps; what is next, and do we follow-up?*

Learning: *What went well? What can I do differently next time?*

IN CONCLUSION

Ask yourself – did I apply the 3 R's of successful coaching conversations?

Did I Reach out with empathy?

Did I Respond thoughtfully?

Did I Resist providing immediate solutions?

©Anton van der Walt

When you have the conversation – use the 3Rs Coaching Conversation Tool

The 3Rs Coaching Conversation Tool consists of three important steps – **Reach Out**, **Respond**, **and Resist** – designed to enhance the quality and effectiveness of coaching conversations. By integrating these principles into your leadership style, you can facilitate more impactful discussions, build stronger relationships, and foster a more engaged and proactive team.

THE 3 R'S COACHING CONVERSATION TOOL

REACH-OUT
Reach out with empathy

How to have
an effective
Coaching
Conversation

RESIST
Resist providing solutions

RESPOND
Respond thoughtfully

Adapted from Centre for Creative Leadership - How to have a coaching conversati

Here's how the tool works:

1. **Reach out with empathy**: This first step calls for leaders to engage their team members with genuine empathy. This involves active listening and a focus on asking thoughtful questions to truly understand their team members' perspectives. Leaders should aim to grasp what their team members are thinking, feeling, saying, and doing. This empathetic approach helps establish a safe, open environment conducive to meaningful dialogue.

2. **Respond thoughtfully**: This second step revolves around thoughtful, considered responses. Rather than offering immediate feedback or ideas, leaders should take the time to carefully consider the issue at hand and formulate a thoughtful, impactful response. This strategy respects the individual's input and encourages more open, honest conversations.

3. **Resist providing immediate solutions**: The final step requires a paradigm shift in many leaders' approaches. It suggests resisting the instinct to provide immediate solutions.

> The 3Rs Coaching Conversation Tool offers a practical framework to enhance coaching conversations.

As leaders, it's often tempting to jump into problem-solving mode. However, coaching is more about guiding team members to find their own solutions, thereby fostering critical thinking skills, autonomy, and self-confidence.

The 3Rs Coaching Conversation Tool offers a practical framework to enhance coaching conversations. By adopting these practices, leaders can facilitate more engaging, productive conversations that foster growth, development, and engagement within their teams.

> *'One of the biggest values of 1:1s is discovering where employees are struggling or stuck and helping them find a path forward. Not by telling them how you'd do it, but by guiding them to come up with their own solution.'*
>
> – Jon Plax, Senior Director, Customer Centric Engineering, Salesforce[28]

Being a leader-coach can be one of the most rewarding and impactful roles in a professional setting. By shifting from a directive, controlling style to a coaching approach, you unlock the potential of your team members and build a high-performance culture that not only delivers stellar results but also fosters an engaged, satisfied, and fulfilled workforce.

The Power of Storytelling: Inspiring and Leading with Impactful Narratives

'No tribal chief or elder has ever handed out statistical reports, charts, graphs, or lists to explain where the group is headed or what it must do.'

– Peg Neuhauser, Author &
Business Consultant[29]

Storytelling is an essential element for impactful leadership. In fact, telling a compelling story is how you build credibility for your ideas, messages and even yourself.[30] However, it's not always easy to balance conveying the messages we need to get across, while also utilising the power of storytelling.

The dilemma of data – the challenge of conveying messages

In the realm of leadership, we often find ourselves at crossroads where we must inspire our teams to take action. Traditionally, leaders have relied heavily on factual data, presentations laden with graphs, spreadsheets, bullet points, and lengthy explanations of gaps and targets. This 'more data equals more understanding' approach, while theoretically compelling, often fails to achieve the desired engagement or impact.

On the other hand, inspiration and motivation can arise through the power of storytelling, showcasing to leaders the need to incorporate this element into their leadership strategy. So, the challenge lies in balancing the requirement to convey essential information against the risk of disengagement or indifference.

The compelling case for storytelling

The reality is that raw data, no matter how essential, can often be unengaging and challenging to connect with emotionally. Instead of saturating our teams with more data in the hope of inspiring action, we need to consider a different approach – one that makes our messages more memorable, clear, relatable, and impactful, and inspires the listener to take action.[31] That's where the power of storytelling comes in.

Data has its place in the story – but it's not the story itself. It serves as supporting evidence, adding credibility and context. The key lies in blending data and the narrative. Create an inspiring story by integrating personal experiences, examples from other companies or leaders, and real-world challenges and solutions. Weaving a narrative around these elements can create a compelling story that resonates on a personal level and inspires action.

Connecting with the human heart – the role of emotional engagement in storytelling

The effectiveness of storytelling lies in its ability to connect with people on an emotional level. Starting with an overview of the 'big idea', followed by a discussion of the challenges we're facing, can foster a sense of shared understanding and mutual acknowledgement. It makes people feel seen and heard, increasing their engagement and investment in the journey ahead.

Always make new mistakes

I would often tell a story in my speaking and leadership engagements, that highlighted the importance of allowing our employees the space to be innovative and come up with new ideas:

'I remember when I was promoted to a challenging and very demanding position. My mentor at the time gave me an extraordinary gift. She gave me a card to pin on my white board with the following inscription: "Always make new mistakes". This left an indelible impression on me because it is only through going outside of your own comfort zone and taking risks, that we learn and grow. More often than not, we encounter resistance and challenges, but by persevering, putting ourselves out there, we learn and grow. Only by stretching ourselves to the limit do we know just how far we can go.

One afternoon as I stood on the windy cliffs overlooking a stormy sea-scape, I noticed how the clouds had opened and the sun was streaming through. This made me think of the late Leonard Cohen's song – "Anthem". In it he said, "There is a crack in everything, that's how the light gets in." Nothing truly beautiful is perfect. It is the flaw that makes us unique and it is the flaw that is the mark of human inspiration. We may not always succeed, but we are nothing if we have not even tried.

There is a 500-year-old Japanese art form called Kintsugi. It is the art of recognising beauty in broken things. Kintsugi is the method of restoring a broken piece of porcelain with lacquer mixed with gold. This art conveys a philosophy not of replacement, but of awe, reverence, and restoration. The gold-filled cracks are testament to its history. The Kintsugi craftsman would say, "It is one beautiful way of living, that you fix your dish by yourself."

Great leaders will give their people the space and time in which to grow and develop. They allow and encourage employees to make new mistakes as they grow and find their feet. Sometimes cracks appear and fixing is required. This is all accepted as part of the growth process.'

A visual journey – using imagery to illustrate the path ahead

An integral part of storytelling in leadership is showing. Providing a visual representation of our current status and future aspirations can help make the journey ahead more tangible and meaningful. This could be as simple as 'We are here today, we need to be there tomorrow,' depicted through compelling visual imagery.

A VISUAL JOURNEY OF THE PATH AHEAD

When you create a visual component to support your 'story', your message becomes more memorable and easier for others to buy-in and take action on.

A 4-step blueprint for effective storytelling

1. **Identify your 'big idea'**: Begin with the core message

or goal that you want your team to understand and commit to.

2. **Acknowledge the challenges**: Discuss the obstacles your team is facing. Show empathy and understanding, creating an emotional connection.

3. **Paint a picture of the future**: Provide a visual representation of where you are and where you aim to be. This helps your team see the journey and destination.

4. **Weave your story**: Integrate personal experiences, relatable examples, and data to create a compelling narrative that inspires and engages.

> By incorporating storytelling into your leadership approach, you can connect more deeply with your team and inspire them to move forward towards your shared goals.

Remember, as a leader your job is to inspire and lead the way. A good story that resonates with your team can be a more potent tool than a slide deck full of bullet points. By incorporating storytelling into your leadership approach, you can connect more deeply with your team and inspire them to move forward towards your shared goals.

The 10% Differentiator in Action

Influencing and inspiring your team is important for growing potential and for becoming a leader that fully embraces your 10% Differentiator. How does this look in action?

The pillars of effective collaboration, and purposeful communication: lessons from coaching with Ahmed Jumah

'In our sessions, I've come away with two main insights: the importance of better task prioritization and gaining a clearer vision of our working methods. Having a clear vision means I'm not just focused on our end goals, but I'm also paying attention to the ways we're achieving those goals. The guidance from these sessions acts as a roadmap, leading me toward improved decision-making and more effective work methods.

Another key realization has been the role of individual values in our team. At first, it might have seemed like a minor detail, but now I see it as a central part of how our team functions together. Recognizing and respecting these values has given me a fresh perspective, enabling me to approach challenges from multiple angles. This ensures that I'm always considering various viewpoints and not overlooking valuable insights.

An invaluable lesson from our sessions is the power of asking the right questions. It's easy to jump to conclusions or make assumptions, but taking a moment to delve deeper can reveal that the real issue might be different from what we first thought. By identifying the heart of the matter, I can then tailor our solutions to be more effective and lasting.

To sum up, a big part of my learning journey is recognizing the importance of active listening. Instead of just putting our ideas forward, taking the time to genuinely understand others' thoughts and feelings makes a world of difference. This not only promotes a collaborative environment but also ensures that our solutions are comprehensive, taking into account the richness of diverse opinions.'

Ahmed Jumah – Managing Director

Key takeaways from Ahmed are:

- **Task prioritisation**: Recognising the significance of organising tasks effectively for optimal results.
- **Clear vision of work methods**: It's essential not just to know our goals, but also to understand the methods we use to achieve them.
- **Role of individual values**: Understanding and

respecting team members' personal values enhances teamwork and collaboration.

- **Multiple perspectives**: Embracing various viewpoints ensures comprehensive solutions and prevents overlooking essential details.

- **Asking the right questions**: Before addressing problems, ensure they're the real issues and not just symptoms or misconceptions.

- **Active listening**: Taking the time to genuinely understand others' thoughts and feelings promotes better collaboration and richer solutions.

Conclusion

Increasing your performance and skills as a leader, and for your team, involves being coachable, being able to coach well, and using storytelling to support your messaging. But by developing these skills you'll also be developing that additional capacity that you need to move beyond the 'adequate' level to the 'excellent' level and create the connection that leads to true productivity and high performance.

Connection

In this book we've talked about many elements of growth. We've talked about Change, and how it can be effectively and compassionately managed while driving productivity. We've discussed the importance of Culture, both a productive and diverse culture within your teams and organisation, and a culture of responsibility within your own leadership.

We've talked about Balance, and the need for a resonant and integrated work-life balance that increases your productivity and wellbeing, as well as how to embrace feedback and lead from behind. We've spoken about Values – learning how to read a room, prioritise what is important to yourself and your organisation, and the importance of seeking alignment with shared values. We've also touched on Potential – how to increase productivity while breaking free of self-limiting beliefs that might encumber you.

Finally, we've discussed Leadership and Influence. With Leadership, we focused on the power of empathetic leadership and the difference between control and influence of others (and what works best). This led us ultimately into Influence, where we covered the benefits of being coachable, coaching others, and the power of storytelling to drive buy-in and action and, at the end of the day, potential.

Implementing the skills around each of these elements – Change, Culture, Balance, Values, Potential, Leadership, and Influence – will see you making incredible strides towards higher performance and better outcomes. However, utilising them all will allow you to transcend the realm of what is familiar, predictable, and 'good enough' to the transformative territory of the 10% Differentiator.

However, to do that we need to understand the final element of the 10% Differentiator – that is building relationships. This element is the one that allows you to connect the dots between every other aspect and be ready to truly embrace your potential.

Connecting the Dots: How Building Relationships Gets Stuff Done

*'You are the average of
the five people you spend
the most time with.'*

– Jim Rohn

The underpinning tenet of productivity, in both personal and professional landscapes, is our ability to nurture healthy relationships. The adage, 'No man is an island,' signifies the collective web of human interaction and reliance. The lone wolf mentality, where you regard yourself as the only trustworthy and reliable entity, is not conducive to a healthy business environment, or to creating a high-performing team that embraces its potential. Even if it's comforting to solely rely on yourself, the undeniable truth is that the world doesn't just consist of ourselves.

> The underpinning tenet of productivity, in both personal and professional landscapes, is our ability to nurture healthy relationships.

The crossroads of success: building beneficial relationships

Relationships aren't a one-way street. Their beauty lies in the mutual exchange of respect, understanding, and assistance. It's not a take-and-give scenario; rather, it's a dance of reciprocity where both parties benefit. Nothing is accomplished in isolation; all things are based on our basic human interactions.

Even a successful person, regardless of the sphere they are in, is continuously in a position of reliance on others. Whether it's a barista making your daily brew, a colleague delivering an essential report, or a family member offering emotional support, our lives are interconnected in ways that necessitate trust in others. This connectedness leads to the realisation that relationship-building is not just a nice-to-have, but rather a must-have, skill.

The obvious inclination when forging connections might be to focus on those who seem to offer the most substantial immediate benefits – your peers, superiors, or anyone at the same level or higher. Building relationships along this line certainly holds importance, but it is crucial not to neglect those seemingly on the periphery of your life.

My personal experience with travel has shown me the value of maintaining relationships beyond the conventional confines. Staying in hotels and traveling between countries, I've encountered the everyday heroes of hospitality: the drivers, the housekeeping staff, and laundry workers.

These individuals might seem to occupy minor roles in the grand scheme of our lives, but they are the uncelebrated, essential pillars that hold up our every comfort and convenience. Without them, we would not be in a position to carry out our highly demanding jobs.

The path forward: broadening the circle of relationships

Ultimately, the quality of our output, the depth of our success, and the enrichment of our lives are all tethered to our ability to build and maintain relationships. The magic truly begins to unfold when we broaden our circle of relationships, transcending biases about who we deem important or likable. Relationships ignite the engine of accomplishment. The path to 'getting stuff done' is not a solitary journey but a shared expedition, navigated through the map of relationships.

The 10% Differentiator in Action

Building relationships is important to get things done, and to embrace your 10% Differentiator. How does this look in action?

It's all in the relationships: lessons from coaching with Sanjay Nigam

'In today's business realm, it often feels like we're navigating uncharted waters, with only about 10% of our journey foreseeable. It's akin to facing unpredictable academic challenges where our preparedness only takes us so far. And when variables come into play, be it from human interactions or unpredictable events, that's where our true test begins.

Handling varying cultural dynamics, international assignments, and the diverse human element changes the content and approach of our dealings significantly. And here's the crux: successful leadership isn't just about understanding these dynamics. It's about effectively pulling all stakeholders into a cohesive unit, resolving conflicts, and ensuring benefits flow through the system.

Consider the multifaceted challenges I face: aligning finance with strategy, getting clearance from business to legal, all while racing against the clock. It's an *intricate ballet of coordination, alignment, and above all, relationships. And these aren't just relationships of convenience; they are genuine connections with every player in the ecosystem. From the finance team to the hotel staff who handle my daily needs – everyone holds importance. It's these connections that can come to our aid during pressing times.*

However, in this whirlwind of efforts, relationships, and alignments, I've realized that there's an element of unpredictability. Despite our best intentions and efforts, uncertainties loom. This calls for an acceptance of what we cannot change, and more so, a humility in recognizing that not all successes and failures fall squarely on our shoulders. Sometimes, external factors play a bigger role.

In essence, success in this landscape is about striking the right balance between preparation and adaptability, between leadership and humility, and between building strategic relationships and fostering genuine connections. As we thread this intricate web, we must remember that every individual, every interaction, and every challenge offers us a chance to learn, adapt, and grow.'

Sanjay Nigam – CEO Automotive

Key takeaways from Sanjay are:

1. **Navigating unpredictability**: Business environments are like uncharted waters with a large portion being unforeseen. Challenges often arise spontaneously, beyond what we've prepared for.

2. **The importance of adaptability**: Navigating diverse cultural dynamics and international assignments requires flexibility. Unpredictable events and human interactions test our adaptability.

3. **Leadership through stakeholder unit**: Success hinges on uniting all stakeholders, from finance to legal. Resolving conflicts and ensuring benefits are key leadership challenges.

4. **Value of relationships**: Genuine connections across the business ecosystem are paramount. Relationships are not just strategic but should be fostered at every level. Building bridges even in unforeseen places can prove beneficial during pressing times.

5. **Facing uncertainties with acceptance**: Despite all efforts, there are always unpredictable elements. Recognising and accepting what's beyond one's control is crucial.

6. **The role of humility**: Successes and failures aren't solely due to individual efforts; external factors can play a significant role. Leaders should remain grounded, recognising the broader forces at play.

7. **Balancing strategy and genuine connections**: While strategic relationships are vital, genuine connections across all tiers provide a more holistic network. Every interaction offers an opportunity to learn and grow.

Paying It Forward

I shall never forget a conversation I once had with a senior executive I coached. He shared a quote which remains with me always: 'The service we render to others is the rent we pay for our room on this earth.'

> 'The service we render to others is the rent we pay for our room on this earth.'

While many attribute this quote to the famed Muhammad Ali from the 70s, its true roots lie with Sir Wilfred Thomas Grenfell, a pioneering British doctor who worked diligently in Labrador, Canada during the late 19th and early 20th centuries. This quote captures the true meaning of leadership.

My coaching methodology with executives has a familiar rhythm. We begin by focusing on the individual: their self-awareness, their driving forces, and potential pitfalls. We dive deep into understanding their personality traits – what invigorates them and what drains them. A pivotal part of our journey is delving into emotional intelligence. It's paramount for a successful leader to recognise and harness this awareness.

As we navigate through the nuances of leadership, reflecting on the differentiators previously discussed in this book, our focus often broadens. Conversations shift to their teams, their corporate culture, and the engagement levels of employees. A deeper understanding ensues.

A pertinent question often emerges: 'Once we are armed with this newfound knowledge and self-awareness, what's next?' This brings us back to Grenfell's insightful quote. Once we've honed our leadership, understood our strengths and areas of growth, the next step is evident. It's time to pay it forward.

There's an unparalleled joy in mentoring and guiding another individual. The investment of your time in such endeavours not only benefits the mentee but often brings unexpected insights and growth to the mentor as well. The real challenge for leaders isn't just personal development. It's about what you give back. The ultimate reward isn't in self-growth alone, but in witnessing the growth of others.

As leaders, our mission is twofold: become an exceptional leader, while guiding others on their journey towards success.

Our legacy can never just be about our own personal accomplishments, instead, it is all about the difference we have made in the lives of those around us. How much growth have we created within ourselves? How much value have we truly added for others?

When we can answer this in a way that resonates within ourselves, then we'll know we've achieved the 10% Differentiator.

Work with Anton

Anton van der Walt, a renowned Keynote Speaker, mentor and coach with a deep understanding of HR and leadership. As the CEO of ROIDEA, his main goal is straightforward: help organisations foster a better culture and enable teams to achieve their best.

With over 25 years of real-world corporate experience from various parts of the globe, Anton knows the ins and outs of leadership. He believes in the power of genuine connection and in unlocking the inherent leadership qualities in everyone.

Anton has authored 3 books, offering insights from his vast experience. Beyond speaking at conferences, he's hands-on, running practical workshops, leadership programmes, and providing one-on-one coaching. He has a special interest in guiding Executive leaders, helping them grow both personally and professionally.

At the core of his work, Anton believes that people make businesses succeed. Simple as that.

Corporate clients have included:
Ford Motor Company ME and South Africa, Petromin Corporation in Saudi Arabia, Nissan Motor Company, ASI Financial Services, Heineken, Virbac, Netstar Australia and South Africa.

Book in a time to chat here https://calendly.com/antonvanderwalt/complimentary-discussion-30-mins or email Anton's team at hello@roidea.io

Alternatively jump on Anton's website at www.antonvanderwalt.com or www.roidea.io to find out about his workshops, speaking and coaching programs.

Other titles by Anton:
Leadership Through My Lens
The Transformational Leader

References

1. Sadun, R., Fuller, J., Hansen, S. & Neal, P.J. (July-August 2022). 'The C-Suite Skills That Matter Most.' *Harvard Business Review*. Available at https://hbr.org/2022/07/the-c-suite-skills-that-matter-most

2. Lewin, K. (1947). 'Frontiers in group dynamics: Concept, Method and Reality in Social Science; Social Equilibria and Social Change.' *Human Relations*. Available at https://journals.sagepub.com/doi/10.1177/001872674700100103.

3. Kotter, J. (2012). *Leading Change*. Harvard Business Review Press.

4. Boulding. B. (16 July 2019). 'For Leaders, Decency Is Just as Important as Intelligence.' *Harvard Business Review*. Available at https://hbr.org/2019/07/for-leaders-decency-is-just-as-important-as-intelligence.

5. Ficarra L., Rubino, M.J. & Morote, E.S. (2020). 'Does Organizational Culture Affect Employee Happiness?' *Journal for Leadership and Instruction*. Available at https://files.eric.ed.gov/fulltext/EJ1282787.pdf.

6. Seppälä E. & Cameron, K. (1 December 2015). 'Proof That Positive Work Cultures Are More Productive.' *Harvard Business Review*. Available at https://hbr.org/2015/12/proof-that-positive-work-cultures-are-more-productive.

7. Kontoghiorghes, C. (October 2015). 'Linking high performance organizational culture and talent management: satisfaction/motivation and organizational commitment as mediators.' *The International Journal of Human Resource Management*. Available at https://www.researchgate.net/publication/282797092_

Linking_high_performance_organizational_culture_and_talent_
management_satisfactionmotivation_and_organizational_
commitment_as_mediators.

8. Rebelo, T. & Gomes, A.D. (July 2017). 'Is organizational learning
   culture a good bet? An analysis of its impact on organizational
   profitability and customer satisfaction.' *Academia Revista
   Latinoamericana de Administración.* Available at https://www.
   researchgate.net/publication/318222182_Is_organizational_
   learning_culture_a_good_bet_An_analysis_of_its_impact_on_
   organizational_profitability_and_customer_satisfaction.

9. Hewson, M. (19 October 2016). 'The 4 Traits You Need to
   Be a Great Leader.' *Fortune.* Available at https://fortune.
   com/2016/10/18/mpw-leadership-lockheed-martin/.

10. Rani, S. & Mariappan, S. (March 2011). 'Work/life balance
    reflections on employee satisfaction.' *Serbian Journal of
    Management.* Available at https://www.researchgate.net/
    publication/50373244_Worklife_balance_reflections_on_
    employee_satisfaction.

11. Satell, G. & Windschitl, C. (11 May 2021). 'High-Performing Teams
    Start with a Culture of Shared Values.' *Harvard Business Review.*
    Available at https://hbr.org/2021/05/high-performing-teams-
    start-with-a-culture-of-shared-values.

12. National Australia Bank. Annual Review 2018: We back the
    bold who move Australia forward. [Report]. Available at https://
    www.nab.com.au/content/dam/nabrwd/documents/reports/
    corporate/2018-annual-review-accessible-version.docx.

13. Knight, R. (10 May 2018). 'Tips for Reading the Room Before a
    Meeting or Presentation'. *Harvard Business Review.* Available
    at https://hbr.org/2018/05/tips-for-reading-the-room-before-a-
    meeting-or-presentation.

14. Celestine, N. (24 November 2015). 'How to Change Self-Limiting Beliefs According to Psychology.' *Positive Psychology*. Available at https://positivepsychology.com/false-beliefs/.

15. Rhodes, J. & Grover, J. (26 June 2023). 'How to Overcome Self-Limiting Beliefs.' *Harvard Business Review*. Available at https://hbr.org/2023/06/how-to-overcome-self-limiting-beliefs.

16. 'The Work is a Practice'. The Work of Byron Katie. Available at https://thework.com/instruction-the-work-byron-katie/.

17. Celestine, N. 'How to Change Self-Limiting Beliefs According to Psychology.'

18. Finerman, A. (19 November 2019). 'The Impact of Limiting Beliefs.' *Wharton Magazine*. Available at https://magazine.wharton.upenn.edu/digital/the-impact-of-limiting-beliefs/.

19. Celestine, N. 'How to Change Self-Limiting Beliefs According to Psychology.'

20. Luft, J. (1970). *Group processes: An introduction to group dynamics*. National Press Books.

21. Van Bommel, T. (2021). *The power of empathy in times of crisis and beyond*. Catalyst.

22. Forbes Coaches Council. (29 December 2017). 'If You Want To Be 'CEO Material,' Develop These 15 Traits.' *Forbes*. Available at https://www.forbes.com/sites/forbescoachescouncil/2017/12/29/if-you-want-to-be-ceo-material-develop-these-15-traits/?sh=783e6efe4ed3.

23. Scales, E. (August 2022). 'The perception of ego in leader-follower dynamics.' [Dissertation, Master of Business Administration, National College of Ireland.] Available at https://norma.ncirl.ie/5814/1/elizabethscales.pdf.

24. Beck, R. & Harter, J. (21 April 2015). 'Managers Account for 70% of Variance in Employee Engagement.' *Gallup Business Journal*. Available at https://news.gallup.com/businessjournal/182792/managers-account-variance-employee-engagement.aspx.

25. Beck, J & Harter, J. 'Managers Account for 70% of Variance in Employee Engagement.'

26. Ibarra, H. & Scoular, A. (November-December 2019). 'The Leader as Coach.' *Harvard Business Review*. Available at https://hbr.org/2019/11/the-leader-as-coach.

27. Schultz, J. (21 January 2021). 'What Is Coaching in the Workplace and Why Is It Important?' *Positive Psychology*. Available at https://positivepsychology.com/workplace-coaching/.

28. Leadr Team. (14 November 2019). 'How-to Guide: The One to One Meeting.' leadr. Available at https://blog.leadr.com/how-to-guide-one-on-one-meeting.

29. Choy, E. (9 September 2021). 'Business Storytelling Culture Can Improve Your Organization In 3 Big Ways.' *Forbes*. Available at https://www.forbes.com/sites/estherchoy/2021/09/19/business-storytelling-culture-can-improve-your-organization-in-3-big-ways/.

30. Gothelf, J. (19 October 2020). 'Storytelling Can Make or Break Your Leadership.' *Harvard Business Review*. Available at https://hbr.org/2020/10/storytelling-can-make-or-break-your-leadership.

31. Decker, A. (2023). 'The Ultimate Guide to Storytelling.' Hubspot. Available at https://blog.hubspot.com/marketing/storytelling.

Printed in Great Britain
by Amazon

30589011R00126